THE
INSTANT KITCHEN
COOKBOOK

Fast and Easy Family Meals Using Your
INSTANT POT® and AIR FRYER

COCO MORANTE

HARVEST
An Imprint of WILLIAM MORROW

HarperCollins books may be purchased for
educational, business, or sales promotional use.
For information, please email the Special Markets
Department at SPsales@harpercollins.com.

FIRST EDITION

Designed by Shubhani Sarkar

Photography © 2022 by Dana Gallagher

Library of Congress Cataloging-in-Publication Data
has been applied for.

ISBN 978-0-06-323589-2

22 23 24 25 26   TC   10 9 8 7 6 5 4 3 2 1

TO MY PORTLAND MAMAS AND THEIR FAMILIES,
WHO INSPIRED ME TO WRITE THIS COOKBOOK

CONTENTS

CHAPTER 6
Main Dishes

CHAPTER 7
Breads, Grains & Pasta

CHAPTER 8
Vegetable Dishes

CHAPTER 9
Sweet Treats

INTRODUCTION

As a cookbook author, I've always tried to give you, the home cook, tools to help you create wholesome, easy-to-prepare meals for your family. This book is my favorite one yet, as the recipes take advantage of not just one great appliance, but two of my favorite kitchen helpers: an Instant Pot and an air fryer. Whether used separately or together, they're my go-to methods of preparation for quick and delicious food.

At the top of each recipe page, you'll notice icons of the Instant Pot, toaster oven–style air fryer, and/or basket-style air fryer. Some recipes make use of an Instant Pot and an air fryer, and for those, you can use either kind of air fryer, so all the icons are included. Instant Pot–only recipes have the Instant Pot icon, and air fryer recipes have either both or one of the air fryer icons. (There are just a couple recipes that work best in a toaster oven–style air fryer, while most will work for either type.) In the recipe instructions, I've done my best to make it very clear when slightly different methods or equipment are needed depending on which sort of air fryer you have.

This book is organized around mealtimes, which truly reflects the way we eat in my home. You'll find chapters for breakfasts, lunches and snacks, dinners, and desserts, plus go-tos for when you want to make one dish and call it a meal. When you want a comforting soup or stew on a chilly day, for lunch or dinner, look to chapters 3 and 4. (The soup chapter includes recipes for crunchy toppings you can make in the air fryer, too, such as croutons, tortilla strips, and cheese crisps.) To put together a meal that consists of one air fryer dish and one Instant Pot dish, head to the main dishes and sides in chapters 6, 7, and 8.

While my family eats an omnivorous diet, we do include a lot of plant-based foods in our weekly lineup. The majority of the recipes in this book are either vegetarian as is or include vegetarian/vegan substitutions. Whether you use ground beef and dairy cheese or their plant-based versions, recipes like Helpful Hamburger with Chickpea Macaroni and Cheddar (page 127) will provide satisfaction and comfort. Plenty of dishes are vegetarian without the use of meat substitutes as well, including Black-Eyed Pea Succotash Stew (page 94).

With a busy household to run, I don't have time for cooking that's fussy, overly complicated, or time-consuming. As such, you'll find that all the recipes in this book are as streamlined as possible, taking advantage of speedy appliances and simple techniques. Pressure cooking will always be a staple around here, especially with recipes that can be made the night before, such as Overnight Steel-Cut Oats (page 2), or soups and stews that hold up well on the "Keep Warm" setting for hours if need be. And whether I'm using a basket-style or toaster oven–style air fryer, I take advantage of the incredibly short preheat time and reduced cook times versus using a conventional oven.

Combining make-ahead and make-it-fast methods is my strategy for feeding my family well, and I think it's a good one! Whether I need to fly by the seat of my pants on a Tuesday night or I've got an impatient toddler asking for breakfast right now, the recipes in this book have gotten me through busy weeks, time and time again. I've also included a sample weekday meal plan to help illustrate how this all works in practice, complete with a shopping list.

Before we dive into the recipes, I'll go over some of the basics of air frying and pressure cooking, tell you all about my must-have tools and accessories, and take you on a tour of my pantry of ingredients I keep on hand for fast and easy cooking.

AIR FRYER BASICS

BASKET-STYLE VERSUS TOASTER OVEN–STYLE AIR FRYERS

I'll admit it, until recently, I was a bit of a snob about air frying methods. I was convinced that a toaster oven–style air fryer (namely, the Omni, Omni Plus, and Omni Pro models from Instant Brands) was the only way to go for their versatility, capacity, and easy cleanup. There's no extra basket to wash, and you can fit a considerable amount of food into the chrome mesh air frying basket or onto the black enameled cooking pan.

Recently, though, Instant Brands really upped the basket-style air fryer game with their Vortex Plus line. My favorite models are in the generous 6-quart size and feature ClearCook technology—a clear window and a well-placed light—so you can easily see into the air fryer as it's cooking. The nonstick cooking surface eliminates the need for aluminum foil or parchment paper, and a quick soak and a gentle scrub with dish soap (or a trip in the dishwasher) are all it takes to get the tray and basket squeaky clean. There's also an 8-quart model in this line, featuring two side-by-side baskets so you can make a couple of dishes at the same time.

I use both an Omni Plus toaster oven–style air fryer and a Vortex Plus basket-style air fryer on a daily basis (sometimes both at the same time), and they each have their advantages. For baked goods and casseroles baked in Pyrex or metal pans, the Omni air fryer toaster oven, with its top and bottom heating elements and variable convection settings, tends to produce the best results. When I am cooking anything that needs to be heated evenly from the top and bottom and can't be flipped, I use the Omni.

The basket-style air fryer comes in clutch for recipes that are classically made in an air fryer, such as anything with a breading. While some people prefer to cook without the use of nonstick surfaces, I will say that a nonstick tray is a whole lot easier to clean than a chrome mesh basket, especially if your food has stuck on a bit.

COOKING PROGRAMS

The recipes in this book take advantage of a few different cooking programs on the Instant Brands air fryers. You'll find that **AIR FRY**, **BAKE**, and **ROAST** are used most often, with the occasional use of the lower-heat **DEHYDRATE** program for proofing dough. (Of course, you can use this setting to dehydrate foods, too.)

There's not a big difference between the **BAKE** and **ROAST** cooking programs on Instant Brands air fryers. They may have different default temperatures and cook times (which vary by model), but you can easily adjust both up or down as needed for any recipe. The main difference is that the "Turn food" notice will come on during the **ROAST** program, beeping to remind you to flip, shake, or stir your food two-thirds of the way through the cooking time. The **AIR FRY** program has a "Turn food" notice, as well. Since baked goods don't generally require this step, the **BAKE** program doesn't have a "Turn food" notice.

GETTING STARTED

To learn more about the specifics of the cooking programs, capabilities, and setup of your air fryer, I urge you to read the accompanying manual. For instance, some models require a "break in" cooking cycle with no food in the basket, and some do not. It's good to know what you're working with before you begin.

PRESSURE COOKER BASICS

While I grew up with a stovetop pressure cooker, in my adult life, the Instant Pot is the only pressure cooker I will ever use. What can I say, pressure cooking technology has come a long way! With easy, programmable cooking settings, the ability to safely walk away during cooking, and settings that allow you to delay the start of cooking or leave something on a warming setting after it's done, they're the only way to go.

Since their sales began to take off in the mid-2010s, Instant Brands has debuted many different Instant Pot models. They keep on refining and improving their technology as the years go by, with hardly a holiday season passing that doesn't include the launch of one or more new Instant Pots. Rest assured, though, you don't have to upgrade your Instant Pot every year to take advantage of the recipes in this cookbook.

BEST BUDGET INSTANT POT

My favorite budget model that's been around for years is the Instant Pot Duo in the 6-quart size. It will do absolutely everything you need an Instant Pot to do, and it retails for under $80. Most recipes you'll find (including all of mine) are developed for use with this mid-size Instant Pot. While the 3-quart and 8-quart models are suitable for smaller- or larger-batch cooking, respectively, you'll have to scale recipes down or up accordingly.

BEST BOUGIE INSTANT POT

On the slightly pricier, all-the-bells-and-whistles end, the 6-quart Instant Pot Pro Plus (list price $170) features many technological improvements over the Duo line. It's a "smart" cooker, so it coordinates with recipes on the Instant Brands app, allowing you to operate it remotely from your phone. I'll admit, though, that the improvements to the physical design of the pot are what I most appreciate about the Pro Plus. Its inner pot has silicone handles, making it easier to lower and lift it in and out of the housing. The inner pot's interior is flat rather than the slightly convex shape of earlier models, making for a more even sear, as well as even cooking when it comes to small batches of grains and beans. The lid automatically seals when you put it on, so you don't have to remember to have it in its "Sealing" position. The pressure release function is nicer, too. It's fully automated, allowing you to select a quick or natural release ahead of time, and it releases a less concentrated jet of steam than earlier models.

INSTANT POT COOKING PROGRAMS

Whichever model you go with, it will have a **SAUTÉ** program, as well as a **PRESSURE COOK** or **MANUAL** cooking program, which will set you up to cook nearly all of the recipes in this book. A **RICE** setting and a **YOGURT** setting are included on most models, which you'll probably want, too. I hardly ever use more specialized cooking programs than those. (Do note that if you're into sous vide cooking, a lot of the newer models have that functionality, which can eliminate the need for a separate appliance for that. I don't include any sous vide recipes in this cookbook, but I do sometimes prepare steaks and roasts this way. Some newer models have a canning setting as well, for both low and high acid foods.)

RECIPES AND INSTRUCTIONS

My Instant Pot recipes are written with both beginners and old-hat Instant Pot users in mind. I'll tell you what buttons to press at every step, whether to release the pressure right away or wait until it's gone down naturally, and how to add ingredients in just the right way to get great results every time. After all, with many years of Instant Pot recipe development under my belt, I've accumulated a lot of handy tricks and tips!

For a more detailed rundown of the specific programs and capabilities of your Instant Pot as well as instructions for setup, cleaning, and safety procedures, do read the manual before use.

MUST-HAVE TOOLS AND ACCESSORIES

In this cookbook, you'll find that the default instructions for air fryer recipes are for the Omni toaster oven–style air fryer. Most of the air fryer recipes also have alternative instructions for using a basket-style air fryer.

OMNI AIR FRYER TOASTER OVEN ACCESSORIES

If you're using an Omni, you can make most of the recipes in this book using the black enamel cooking pan or the basket included with the appliance. If a recipe uses the **AIR FRY** cooking program, simply put the metal oven rack in the rack position labeled "Air Fry," then place the black enamel cooking pan underneath it in the bottom oven rack position to catch any drips or crumbs. If a recipe uses the **BAKE** program, position the cooking pan in the oven rack position labeled "Bake."

For air fryer recipes that use additional cookware, such as a cake pan or Pyrex baking dish, place the cookware directly on top of the black enamel cooking pan. It provides a much more stable surface than the metal oven rack, which is better suited to air frying and toasting.

To make recipes such as Rocky Road Brownies (page 237) and Mango and Greek Yogurt Cheesecake (page 247), you'll need to use a Pyrex or metal 8-inch square baking dish and a 7-inch springform pan, respectively. These don't come with your appliance, but you may have them in your kitchen already. I also make use of silicone muffin cups for individual servings of Veggie Meatloaf Muffins (page 167). They come in handy for other baked goods, too.

VORTEX BASKET AIR FRYER ACCESSORIES

If you're using a basket-style air fryer, you'll cook all of the recipes directly on the nonstick cooking tray that is included with the appliance. You don't need to line the cooking tray with parchment paper or aluminum foil, which can in fact be a safety hazard in a basket-style air fryer. The nonstick tray and basket are dishwasher safe, but I usually clean mine in the sink with a bit of dish soap and a nonabrasive dish brush or sponge, so they're ready to use again right away. For recipes that require a baking dish such as Focaccia with Zucchini and Cherry Tomatoes (page 187), I use an 8-inch cake pan, which fits perfectly on top of the nonstick cooking tray in the air frying basket.

OIL SPRAYING BOTTLE

Many air fryer recipes make use of sprayable cooking oil. This allows you to get a light coating of oil on the outside of food so it'll crisp up and give a "fried" result without the large amount of oil used in traditional frying. I go back and forth between using avocado and olive oils, depending on the recipe. You can either use refillable spray bottles, such as Evo or Misto brands, or purchase prefilled spray bottles or cans from the grocery store, such as Spectrum, Chosen Foods, Pam, or a store brand.

COOKING UTENSILS

There are a few cooking utensils that I find indispensable for air frying and pressure cooking. Stainless-steel tongs are my preferred tool for tossing, flipping, and grabbing foods. Look for a set with a nonslip grip on the handles for easier and safer operation. A thin, flexible spatula will help with turning foods in any type of air fryer, since you can easily slide the edge of the spatula underneath breaded or otherwise delicate foods. I like the black nylon ones from OXO. Cookie scoops are my preferred tools for portioning out cookie dough, meatballs, and drop biscuits, and I use them in 1½- and 2½-tablespoon sizes, depending on the recipe.

HEAT-RESISTANT MITTS

Safety is top of mind for me when using air fryers and pressure cookers. Heat-resistant mitts provide a layer of protection when you're putting in and removing foods from a hot air fryer. I like to use large oven mitts as opposed to mini mitts, for added protection. When it comes to pressure cooking, wear mitts when you're lowering and lifting your Instant Pot's inner pot in and out of its housing or performing a manual pressure release, which can let out a pretty forceful jet of steam from the pot lid.

STEAM RACKS AND BASKETS

A raised metal steam rack is included with your Instant Pot—this comes in handy for Soft- or Hard-Boiled Eggs (page 13) and other recipes that require food to steam above a small amount of water, such as Seitan and White Bean Chimichurri Sausages (page 171).

One other type of rack I like to use for pressure cooking is a long-handled silicone one. This is the easiest tool for lifting and lowering baking pans in and out of the Instant Pot. Instant Brands refers to theirs as a "bakeware sling."

For steaming bite-size vegetables and other items that would fall through a steam rack, I like to use a wire mesh steamer basket. The ones from Instant Brands come in small and large sizes. If you're going to get just one, go for the large size, which is the most versatile.

THE INSTANT KITCHEN PANTRY

Here are a few pantry items that I always have on hand to make air fryer and pressure cooker recipes.

BREADCRUMBS AND CEREALS

Breadcrumbs perform much better than liquid batters in the air fryer, so they are a go-to solution for achieving crispy "fried" results. My favorite kind to use are panko—they're crunchier and less dense than traditional breadcrumbs, making for extra-crispy Panko Party Wings (page 34).

Breakfast cereals can do double duty as a crunchy coating and a filler or binding agent in recipes. Crushed cornflakes are a retro classic for Crispy Cornflake Chicken or Tofu Tenders (page 149), and you can use either cornflakes or puffed rice cereal in Veggie Meatloaf Muffins (page 167).

BROTH CONCENTRATES, CONDIMENTS, AND SAUCES

I don't often set aside the time to make homemade broths these days, so I rely on high-quality broth concentrates instead. The reduced-sodium ones from Better Than Bouillon are my favorites. They carry beef, chicken, and vegetable broths in their reduced-sodium line, and I use them all on a regular basis, especially when I want to add depth of flavor to soups, stews, and braises.

Strongly flavored condiments and sauces from a variety of global cuisines make regular appearances in my recipes. Whether it's a dollop of black bean garlic sauce for Tofu and Asparagus with Black Bean Garlic Sauce (page 177), a squeeze of gochujang to spice up a katsu dipping sauce for Panko Party Wings (page 34), or a spoonful of Dijon mustard stirred into a pot of Rosemary-Dijon Chicken and Dumplings (page 99) or spread on a Turkey Monte Cristo Sandwich (page 37), condiments with a punch of flavor come in handy when I want to make a tasty meal fast.

DRIED AND CONCENTRATED FRUITS AND VEGETABLES

Dried fruits lend themselves well to pressure cooking, since they absorb liquid and soften as they cook. I love adding raisins or currants to Italian-Style Meatballs (page 161), and one of my favorite simple desserts is Dried Apricot Compote (page 257).

Tomato paste makes its way into a lot of my recipes. It adds depth of flavor, acidity, and a hit of umami, especially in pressure-cooked dishes like soups and chilis in which the liquid won't reduce much during cooking. Just be careful not to stir it in if your cooking liquid is fairly thick, as it can hinder the liquid from boiling rapidly enough to create necessary steam for the pressure to build. You'll notice that much of the time, I'll simply add a dollop of tomato paste on top just before sealing the pot.

FLOUR AND LEAVENING AGENTS

All-purpose flour is used in the breading process for many foods, and I also use it to make a lot of simple baked goods such as Personal Pesto Pizzas (page 51), Two-Ingredient Flatbreads (page 191), and Buttermilk Drop Biscuits with Honey Butter (page 183). To make any recipes that use all-purpose flour into gluten-free ones, I use the gluten-free blends from Cup4Cup, King Arthur Flour, or Bob's Red Mill. Almond and tapioca flour go into my Grain-Free Dinner Rolls (page 185) if I'm cooking a paleo-style meal.

For leavening agents, you'll find the usual suspects in this cookbook: yeast, baking soda, and baking powder. SAF instant yeast is my favorite—it's reliably quick rising and doesn't require blooming in liquid before baking. For baking powder, I like aluminum-free varieties from Rumford and Bob's Red Mill.

GRAINS AND BEANS

Rolled and steel-cut oats are a breakfast staple in my house, either in Granola with Peanuts and Berries (page 26) or Overnight Steel-Cut Oats (page 2). We also eat a fair amount of rice, pasta, and whole grains as side dishes or incorporated into main dishes, soups, and stews. I love the added chew and texture of bulgur in Beef and Bulgur–Stuffed Peppers (page 139), and I often use chickpea-based pastas when I'm making one-pot meals like Helpful Hamburger with Chickpea Macaroni and Cheddar (page 127) for an extra dose of protein and fiber. Canned or dried pinto beans, black beans, and chickpeas are always on hand for Tempeh or

Beef Chili (page 111), Veggie and Black Bean Quesadilla (page 54), and Orzo and Chickpea Pilaf (page 200).

OILS

I try to keep my pantry as streamlined as possible, so for oils, I almost always rely on one of two: avocado oil or extra-virgin olive oil, in both liquid and spray form (see page xiv). Avocado oil has a neutral flavor and a high smoke point, so it's quite versatile—you can use it for searing, sautéing, or spraying on air-fried foods. Extra-virgin olive oil has a stronger flavor that is suited to Mediterranean cuisines, and a little drizzle goes a long way to add richness to my Lemony Farro and Chicken Soup (page 70).

Of course, you can use whatever cooking oil you prefer. Substitute any neutral-flavored vegetable oil with a high smoke point for avocado oil in any of the recipes in this book, if you like. Canola oil, grapeseed oil, and safflower oil will work well. Likewise, if you prefer a less strongly flavored olive oil, feel free to use a milder variety than extra-virgin.

SPICE BLENDS AND RUBS

Like condiments and sauces, spice blends and rubs are one of the easiest ways to incorporate flavor into your dishes. I make my own jerk spice blend for Jerk-Spiced Salmon, Tomatoes, and Sweet Potatoes (page 135), as well as a barbecue rub for BBQ Tempeh or Tofu (page 165). Of course, you can go the fully store-bought route; I use store-bought Italian seasoning, chili powder, seasoned salt, and Old Bay often. When using

just plain salt, I reach for easy-to-find Diamond brand kosher salt. You don't need to have a pantry full of individual or fancy spices to make delicious food.

CHAPTER 1

BREAKFAST

Overnight Steel-Cut Oats

A warm, comforting bowl of oatmeal is one of my favorite breakfasts, especially when there's virtually no cooking involved in the morning. When you use the **Delay Start** function on your Instant Pot, you can set everything up the night before. Once the cooking program is finished in the morning, all that's left is to stir up the oats and serve them with your toppings of choice, such as a splash of half-and-half or milk, a pat of butter, raisins, brown sugar, maple syrup, nut butter, fresh berries, a spoonful of jam, a sprinkle of cinnamon or pumpkin pie spice . . . or, for an extra-special breakfast, pair them with Honey-Roasted Fruit (page 25).

**1½ cups steel-cut oats
(gluten-free if preferred)**

4½ cups water

½ teaspoon kosher salt

NOTE: The oats will stay hot on the **KEEP WARM** setting once the cooking program ends. If they've been sitting in the pot for an hour or two, they may have thickened and set up a bit. Add a splash of water or milk and stir to loosen them up again, as needed.

1. Add the oats, water, and salt to the Instant Pot. Stir to combine.

2. Secure the lid and set the pressure release to **Sealing**. Select the **PRESSURE COOK** or **MANUAL** setting for 12 minutes at high pressure.

3. Set the **Delay Start** function for as many hours as you need— you'll want the cooking program to start about an hour before you want to serve breakfast. For instance, if you're putting your oats in the pot at 8 pm and you want to eat breakfast at 7 am, set the time delay for 10 hours so the oats will start cooking at 6 am.

4. When the cooking program ends, let the pressure release naturally (this will take about 30 minutes). Open the pot and stir in any liquid sitting on top of the oats.

5. Serve the oats with your favorite toppings.

Dairy-Free (if modified), PREP TIME: **5 MINUTES**   COOK TIME: **45 MINUTES**   YIELD: **4 SERVINGS**
Gluten-Free (if modified),
Vegan (if modified)

Grits Two Ways (Savory or Sweet)

Serve up comforting bowls of grits for breakfast, with a savory, jook-inspired topping or a sweet combination of nut butter, bananas, hemp seeds, and honey. This recipe also works with polenta. Just make sure you're using a stone-ground variety of grits or polenta, not one labeled "instant."

GRITS

1 cup stone-ground grits or polenta (not instant)

5 cups water

2 tablespoons butter (dairy or plant-based) or extra-virgin olive oil

½ teaspoon kosher salt

SAVORY TOPPINGS (PER SERVING)

1 teaspoon soy sauce or tamari

1 teaspoon sambal oelek *or* ½ teaspoon sriracha

Toasted sesame oil, for drizzling

½ green onion, thinly sliced (about 1 tablespoon)

4 soft-boiled eggs (page 13, optional)

SWEET TOPPINGS (PER SERVING)

1 tablespoon nut butter (any variety)

½ banana, thinly sliced

1 tablespoon hemp seeds

2 teaspoons honey or agave nectar

1. Add the grits, water, butter, and salt to the Instant Pot. Stir to combine.

2. Secure the lid and set the pressure release to **Sealing**. Select the **PRESSURE COOK** or **MANUAL** setting for 10 minutes at high pressure. (The pot will take about 15 minutes to come to pressure before the cooking program begins.)

3. When the cooking program ends, let the pressure release naturally for at least 20 minutes, then move the pressure release to **Venting** to release any remaining steam. Open the pot and use a whisk to break up any lumps and incorporate any liquid sitting on top of the grits.

4. Serve the grits with your choice of savory or sweet toppings.

NOTE: I don't use the **Delay Start** function with grits or polenta, as they tend to turn out with more lumps when they're soaked ahead of cooking.

Dairy-Free (if modified), Gluten-Free, Vegan (if modified)   PREP TIME: **5 MINUTES**   COOK TIME: **40 MINUTES**   YIELD: **4 TO 6 SERVINGS**

Teff Porridge

If you'd like to switch up your usual breakfast, teff porridge is a wonderfully nutritious gluten-free option that's high in fiber and protein. The tiny grains cook up in minutes, and the resulting porridge has a slightly nutty, toasty flavor. The options for toppings are pretty much endless—I've listed my go-tos here so that you can pick and choose to make a favorite bowl of your own.

1½ cups whole-grain teff

5 cups water

2 tablespoons butter (dairy or plant-based)

½ teaspoon kosher salt

FOR SERVING (OPTIONAL)

Fresh berries, sliced bananas, or sliced stone fruit

Pepitas, sliced almonds, or hemp seeds

Honey, agave nectar, or maple syrup

Ground cinnamon or pumpkin pie spice

Half-and-half or milk (dairy or plant-based)

1. Add the teff, water, butter, and salt to the Instant Pot. Stir to combine.

2. Secure the lid and set the pressure release to **Sealing**. Select the **PRESSURE COOK** or **MANUAL** setting for 8 minutes at high pressure.

3. When the cooking program ends, let the pressure release naturally for at least 20 minutes, then move the pressure release to **Venting** to release any remaining steam. Open the pot and stir in any liquid sitting on top of the teff.

4. Serve the porridge with your choice of toppings.

NOTE: The porridge will stay hot on the **KEEP WARM** setting once the cooking program ends. If it has been sitting in the pot for an hour or two, it may have thickened and set up a bit. Add a splash of water or milk as needed and stir to loosen it to your desired consistency.

Dairy-Free (it modified), Gluten-Free, Vegan (if modified)   PREP TIME: **5 MINUTES**   COOK TIME: **30 MINUTES**   YIELD: **4 SERVINGS**

Buckwheat Breakfast Bowls

It took me many, many attempts to come up with a foolproof method for evenly pressure-cooked, fluffy buckwheat groats (aka kasha). I'm so excited to finally include them in a cookbook, as they're one of my favorite grains (well, technically a pseudocereal). Whether you top them with avocado and tamari, soft-boiled eggs and hot sauce, or milk and honey, they make for a filling and hearty start to the day. Make sure to buy roasted buckwheat groats, rather than the raw variety, for the best flavor and results.

1 tablespoon butter (dairy or plant-based)

1 cup roasted buckwheat groats (kasha)

1½ cups low-sodium vegetable broth *or* 1½ cups water plus ¼ teaspoon kosher salt

SAVORY TOPPINGS (PER SERVING)

½ medium avocado, peeled and sliced

1 teaspoon soy sauce or tamari *or* ½ teaspoon hot sauce (your favorite variety)

1 soft-boiled egg (page 13)

SWEET TOPPINGS (PER SERVING)

½ cup milk (dairy or plant-based)

2 teaspoons honey or agave nectar

1. Select the **SAUTÉ** setting on the Instant Pot and melt the butter.

2. When the butter is melted and bubbling (after a minute or so), add the buckwheat groats to the pot. Sauté for about 2 minutes, stirring constantly, until fragrant. Pour in the broth (for savory buckwheat) or water and salt (to pair with sweet toppings) and stir to combine, making sure all the grains are submerged.

3. Secure the lid and set the pressure release to **Sealing**. Select the **PRESSURE COOK** or **MANUAL** setting for 5 minutes at high pressure. (The pot will take about 5 minutes to come to pressure before the cooking program begins.)

4. When the cooking program ends, let the pressure release naturally for 15 minutes, then move the pressure release to **Venting** to release any remaining steam.

5. Open the pot. Stir and fluff the buckwheat with a fork, then enjoy with the toppings of your choice.

Gluten-Free, Vegetarian   PREP TIME: **5 MINUTES**   COOK TIME: **8 HOURS**   YIELD: **4 TO 6 SERVINGS**
(PLUS 30 MINUTES FOR   **15 MINUTES**
MILK TO COOL)

Yogurt with Chia Berry Jam

Make yogurt in your Instant Pot and enjoy it with a simple, no-cook berry jam. Both the yogurt and jam recipes are mostly hands-off, making them smart additions to a weekend food prep day. Layer the yogurt and jam with fresh berries and Granola with Peanuts and Berries (page 26) for a delicious parfait as pictured here, or make your own "fruit on the bottom" yogurt cups to enjoy throughout the week.

YOGURT

4 cups whole milk

2 tablespoons plain whole-milk yogurt with live active cultures *or* **1 envelope yogurt starter culture**

JAM

1 pint fresh or thawed frozen mixed berries (roughly chopped if using strawberries)

¼ cup agave nectar or honey

1 tablespoon chia seeds

Pinch kosher salt

1. **Make the yogurt:** Add the milk to the Instant Pot. Select the **YOGURT** setting and adjust it to the "High" or "More" setting. Leaving the lid off the pot, let the milk come up to a temperature of 180°F, or scalding hot. The cooking program will either end or switch from "preheating" to "cooking" when it reaches this temperature. (This will take about 15 minutes.) Turn off the pot.

2. Wearing heat-resistant mitts, remove the inner pot from the housing and pour the scalded milk into a 6- or 7-cup Pyrex storage container. Allow the milk to cool down to 115°F when measured with an instant-read thermometer, or until it's lukewarm to the touch. (This will take about 30 minutes.)

3. While the milk is cooling, rinse out the inner pot and place it back in the housing.

4. Once the milk has cooled, whisk in the yogurt until no lumps remain. Place the Pyrex container on top of the wire metal rack, then lower it into the Instant Pot. Place the lid on the Instant Pot. (It doesn't matter whether the lid is in the **Sealing** or **Venting** position.)

(Continued)

NOTE: For extra-creamy yogurt, whisk ¼ cup powdered milk into the milk before heating.

5. Select the **YOGURT** setting once more, then adjust it to the "Low" or "Less" setting. Set the time for 8 hours for mild-flavored yogurt, or 10 or 12 hours for tart or very tart yogurt.

6. When the cooking program ends, cover the Pyrex container and transfer to the refrigerator. Chill for at least 6 hours before serving. The yogurt will keep in the refrigerator for up to 2 weeks.

7. **Make the jam:** In a bowl, combine the berries, agave, chia seeds, and salt. Use a potato masher or fork to mash the berries and stir the mixture together until the berries are mostly mashed (it is fine if some chunky pieces remain) and the chia seeds are distributed evenly throughout. Cover and transfer to the refrigerator to firm up for at least 2 hours, or up to overnight. The jam will keep in a tightly lidded container in the refrigerator for up to 1 week. Stir once more before serving.

Soft- or Hard-Boiled Eggs

Whether you like your eggs soft- or hard-boiled, and whether you want to use an Instant Pot or an air fryer, this recipe is for you. Either method is more hands-off than boiling your eggs on the stove, and both work well. Serve soft-boiled eggs over Buckwheat Breakfast Bowls (page 9) or Grits Two Ways (page 5), chop up hard-boiled eggs for Avocado Egg Salad Sandwiches (page 47), or enjoy them as is for a fast breakfast or snack.

Large eggs (up to 1 dozen)

Instant Pot Method

1. Pour a cup of water into the Instant Pot and place the metal steam rack inside. Place the eggs on the wire metal rack.

2. Secure the lid and set the pressure release to **Sealing**. Select the **PRESSURE COOK** or **MANUAL** setting for 3 minutes for soft-boiled eggs or 6 minutes for hard-boiled eggs. (The pot will take about 10 minutes to come up to pressure before the cooking program begins.)

3. While the eggs are cooking, prepare an ice bath.

4. When the cooking program ends, perform a quick pressure release by moving the pressure release to **Venting**. Open the pot. Use a pair of tongs to transfer the eggs to the ice bath.

5. Once the eggs have cooled (after about 5 minutes), peel and use them right away or store them in the refrigerator for up to 1 week.

(Continued)

Air Fryer Method

1. Preheat the air fryer on **AIR FRY** at 250°F and set the cooking time for 15 minutes for soft-boiled eggs or 20 minutes for hard-boiled eggs.

2. Place the eggs in the air frying basket. Air fry the eggs in the preheated air fryer.

3. While the eggs are cooking, prepare an ice bath.

4. When the cooking program ends, use a pair of tongs to transfer the eggs to the ice bath.

5. Once the eggs have cooled (after about 5 minutes), peel and use them right away or store them in the refrigerator for up to 1 week.

Dairy-Free, Gluten-Free (if modified), Vegan — PREP TIME: **10 MINUTES (PLUS 1 HOUR TO MARINATE)** — COOK TIME: **10 MINUTES** — YIELD: **4 TOASTS PLUS EXTRA TEMPEH BACON**

Avocado Toast with Tempeh Bacon

TEMPEH BACON

3 tablespoons soy sauce or tamari

2 tablespoons maple syrup

1 tablespoon extra-virgin olive oil

1 teaspoon apple cider vinegar

½ teaspoon liquid smoke flavoring or smoked paprika

½ teaspoon freshly ground black pepper

1 (8-ounce) package tempeh (gluten-free if preferred), sliced into ¼-inch-thick strips

TOAST

4 thick slices crusty artisan bread, such as a boule or bâtard, *or* gluten-free bread

2 garlic cloves, peeled and halved

2 tablespoons extra-virgin olive oil

1 large avocado

Salt and pepper, to taste

1. In a shallow bowl or dish, stir together the soy sauce, maple syrup, olive oil, vinegar, liquid smoke, and pepper until evenly combined. Add the tempeh to the marinade, turning each slice to coat on both sides. Cover the bowl and marinate in the refrigerator for at least 1 hour or up to overnight.

2. Preheat the air fryer on **BAKE** at 400°F and set the cooking time for 10 minutes. If using a toaster oven–style air fryer, line the cooking pan with parchment paper.

3. Spread out the tempeh in a single layer in the air frying basket or on the lined cooking pan. Reserve the marinade.

4. Bake the tempeh in the preheated air fryer for 10 minutes.

5. When the cooking program ends, remove the tempeh from the air fryer. (If you want a stronger bacon-y flavor and a bit of a glazy appearance, you can brush a light coat of the marinade on both sides at this point, while the tempeh is still warm.)

6. Toast the bread in the air fryer on the **TOAST** setting. If your model does not have this setting, use the **BROIL** setting at its highest temperature (some will go up to 450°F, while others top out at 400°F) for 3 to 5 minutes, depending on the level of browning you prefer.

(Continued)

NOTES: The longer you marinate the tempeh bacon, the stronger the flavor will be.

For a little spicy kick, substitute hot sauce (such as Frank's RedHot or Tabasco) for the vinegar.

Keep leftover bacon refrigerated in a tightly lidded container for up to 4 days.

7. When the cooking program ends, remove the toast from the air fryer and rub the garlic cloves over the surface of the bread. Drizzle the bread with the olive oil.

8. Halve, pit, and peel the avocado, then halve each half again. Top each slice of toast with one-quarter of the avocado. Use a fork to mash the avocado on top of the toast, then sprinkle with salt and pepper. Top each toast with a few slices of tempeh bacon and serve right away.

Scones Two Ways (Savory or Sweet)

These aren't your average scones. Thanks to the addition of Greek yogurt, they bake up extremely tender and fluffy, almost like a scone-biscuit hybrid. Mix in shredded cheddar and green onions for a savory option, or add chopped strawberries and drizzle with a tangy lime glaze if you're in the mood for something sweet. I like to make the dough the night before, then bake them in the morning for an easy breakfast or brunch treat.

DOUGH

1¼ cups all-purpose flour or gluten-free flour blend

2 tablespoons granulated sugar (only if making sweet scones)

1 teaspoon baking powder

¼ teaspoon baking soda

⅛ teaspoon kosher salt

4 tablespoons cold unsalted butter, cut into ⅓-inch cubes

⅓ cup whole-milk or low-fat Greek yogurt

1 large egg

FOR SAVORY SCONES

½ cup shredded cheddar cheese

¼ cup chopped green onions

FOR SWEET SCONES

6 medium strawberries, cut into ½-inch pieces (½ cup)

½ cup powdered sugar

½ teaspoon grated lime zest

1 tablespoon fresh lime juice

1. In a mixing bowl, combine the flour, sugar (if using), baking powder, baking soda, and salt and stir to combine. Sprinkle in the cubed butter and use a pastry cutter or fork to incorporate the butter into the flour for a couple minutes, until no larger than pea-size chunks of butter remain and the butter has been mostly worked into the flour.

2. In a small bowl, whisk together the yogurt and egg until no streaks remain. Pour the mixture into the bowl with the dry ingredients. Use a silicone spatula to gently mix the wet and dry ingredients, just until all of the flour is absorbed and the dough begins to come away from the sides of the bowl—it will still be a bit crumbly. Fold in the cheese and green onions or the strawberries, just until they are evenly incorporated and the dough is no longer crumbly.

3. Turn the dough out onto a piece of plastic wrap. Pat the dough into a disk, about ½ inch thick and 7 inches across. Top the dough with another piece of plastic wrap, then tuck in the sides. Refrigerate for at least 1 hour, or up to 24 hours. (If you'd like to speed things up, you can freeze the dough for 30 minutes instead.)

(Continued)

4. Preheat the air fryer on **BAKE** at 325°F and set the cooking time for 12 minutes. If using a toaster oven–style air fryer, line the cooking pan with parchment paper.

5. Using a chef's knife or bench scraper, cut the dough disk into eight equal wedges. Place the scones in the air frying basket or on the lined cooking pan, spacing them at least ½ inch apart. Bake the scones in the preheated air fryer.

6. While the scones are baking, if making the sweet version, whisk together the powdered sugar, lime zest, and lime juice in a small bowl. Line a quarter sheet pan with a cooling rack. This is where you'll cool and glaze the scones—the sheet pan is meant to catch any dripping glaze.

7. When the cooking program ends, wearing heat-resistant mitts, remove the basket or cooking pan from the air fryer. Use a thin, flexible spatula to transfer the scones to the cooling rack.

8. If making savory scones, let cool for at least 10 minutes, then enjoy. If making sweet scones, while they are still warm, drizzle each scone with about 1 teaspoon of the glaze. Let cool for at least 10 minutes, then enjoy.

Nut Butter and Banana French Toast Sandwiches

This not-too-sweet stuffed French toast is a breakfast treat that won't get everybody too sugared up. Protein-packed nut butter and cream cheese are mixed together, and you can layer either sliced banana or jam in the middle of the creamy filling.

3 large eggs

1 cup milk

½ teaspoon ground cinnamon

½ teaspoon vanilla extract

4 ounces cream cheese, softened at room temperature

¼ cup peanut butter or other nut butter

8 slices challah bread, Texas toast, or gluten-free bread

1 large ripe banana, cut into thin slices, or 4 tablespoons jam, any variety

Powdered sugar, for serving (optional)

Maple syrup, for serving

1. If using a toaster oven–style air fryer, line the cooking pan with parchment paper.

2. In a shallow bowl, whisk together the eggs, milk, cinnamon, and vanilla. Set aside.

3. In a small bowl, stir together the cream cheese and peanut butter.

4. On a cutting board, spread all the slices of bread with the cream cheese mixture, about 1½ tablespoons per slice. Top four of the slices with banana slices or jam, then sandwich them together with the other slices, to make four sandwiches.

5. Preheat the air fryer on **BAKE** at 375°F and set the cooking time for 8 minutes.

6. When the air fryer has preheated, pick up a sandwich with both hands, dunk it into the egg-milk mixture for 5 seconds, turn it over and dunk the second side, then place it on the lined cooking pan or directly in the basket. Repeat with the rest of the sandwiches.

7. Bake the sandwiches in the preheated air fryer.

8. When the **Turn food** notice comes on (or two-thirds of the way through the cooking time), use a thin, flexible spatula to flip the sandwiches.

9. When the cooking program ends, transfer the sandwiches to serving plates, top with a light dusting of powdered sugar (if using), cut in half, and serve right away, with maple syrup at the table.

Honey-Roasted Fruit

Spooning some warm, honeyed fruit on top of your Overnight Steel-Cut Oats (page 2) or Yogurt with Chia Berry Jam (page 10) is an extra-luxe way to start the day. It's also a smart use of fruits that are looking a little sad in the bottom of the produce drawer. Give them a 10-minute makeover and enjoy. The fruit is also delicious on top of French toast, pancakes, and waffles.

1 pound stone fruit (nectarines, peaches, or plums), pitted and cut into ½-inch pieces

or

1 pound apples or pears, cored and cut into ½-inch pieces

or

1 pound strawberries, quartered (halved if small), or whole blueberries, raspberries, or blackberries

2 tablespoons honey or agave nectar

¼ teaspoon ground cinnamon

1. Preheat the air fryer on **ROAST** at 350°F and set the cooking time to 10 minutes. If using a toaster oven–style air fryer, line the cooking pan with parchment paper.

2. In a bowl, toss the fruit with the honey and cinnamon until evenly combined.

3. Spread out the fruit in the air frying basket or on the lined cooking pan. Roast the fruit in the preheated air fryer.

4. When the cooking program ends, use a spatula to transfer the fruit to serving plates or bowls.

Dairy-Free (if modified),
Gluten-Free (if modified),
Vegan

PREP TIME: **5 MINUTES**   COOK TIME: **20 MINUTES**   YIELD: **ABOUT 4 CUPS**

Granola with Peanuts and Berries

I like my granola deeply browned, not too sweet, and studded with dried or freeze-dried fruits. This peanut butter–flavored version brings to mind the flavors of a PB&J sandwich, just in crunchy cereal form. Serve it on top of any plant-based or dairy yogurt (or my Yogurt with Chia Berry Jam, page 10), layered in a parfait according to the recipe note below, or sprinkled on top of your favorite smoothie.

⅓ cup agave nectar or maple syrup

⅓ cup coconut oil or ghee

¼ cup smooth peanut butter

1 teaspoon vanilla extract

½ teaspoon ground cinnamon

½ teaspoon kosher salt

3 cups old-fashioned oats (gluten-free if preferred)

1 cup freeze-dried or dried strawberries, blueberries, and/or raspberries

NOTE: To make a yogurt parfait: Spoon ¼ cup plain yogurt into a jam jar or drinking glass, followed by 1 tablespoon any jam or fruit spread, ¼ cup berries or chopped fruit, and 2 tablespoons granola. Repeat the layers once more, then serve right away.

1. If using a toaster oven–style air fryer, line the cooking pan with parchment paper. If using a basket-style air fryer, cut a 12-inch square of parchment paper. Press the parchment down into the air frying basket, making sure it goes only a couple inches up the sides. Trim if necessary, then remove the parchment from the air fryer (you don't want it in there during the preheating, as it won't be weighed down).

2. In a small saucepan on the stove over medium-low heat, or in a microwave-safe bowl in the microwave for 15-second intervals, heat the agave nectar, coconut oil, and peanut butter, stirring often, just until the oil and peanut butter have melted and everything is warmed through and evenly mixed. Turn off the heat and stir in the vanilla, cinnamon, and salt.

3. Preheat the air fryer on **BAKE** at 300°F and set the cooking time for 18 minutes.

4. Add the oats to a mixing bowl. Pour the warm agave–peanut butter mixture over the oats. Working quickly, before the oats can absorb the wet ingredients, use a silicone spoon or spatula to stir until the oats are evenly coated.

5. If using a toaster oven–style air fryer, spread out the mixture in an even layer on the lined cooking pan. If using a basket-style air fryer, place the parchment in the basket, then add the granola and spread it out in an even layer.

6. Bake the granola in the preheated air fryer, stirring every 6 minutes or so (twice during baking) to ensure even browning.

7. When the cooking program ends, let the granola cool to room temperature on the pan or in the air frying basket (about 45 minutes). Break up the granola into clumps as small as you like, then stir in the dried berries.

8. Enjoy right away, or transfer to a tightly lidded container and store at room temperature for up to 2 weeks.

CHAPTER 2

LUNCH & SNACK TIME

Dairy-Free (if modified), Gluten-Free, Vegan (if modified)   PREP TIME: **10 MINUTES**   COOK TIME: **5 MINUTES**   YIELD: **2 TO 4 SERVINGS**

Nacho Scoops with Avocado Crema

These vegetarian nachos make a fun and fast meal for two or a snack for four. Each individual chip is loaded up with toppings, so no bare chips are in sight! My favorite chips to use for nachos are Tostitos Scoops—each one is a self-contained, perfect bite. Topped with avocado crema rather than sour cream, the nachos are easily made vegan by subbing in plant-based cheese shreds for dairy cheese. Use any extra crema on Chicken or Soy Curl Fajitas (page 130) or other Mexican-inspired meals.

NACHO SCOOPS

20 tortilla "scoops" or round chips

½ cup cooked or canned black beans, drained and rinsed

¼ cup sliced black olives

20 pickled jalapeño chile slices *or* 1 jalapeño chile, thinly sliced

⅔ cup shredded Mexican cheese blend (dairy or plant-based)

CREMA

¼ cup avocado oil

2 tablespoons water

2 tablespoons fresh lime juice

1 medium avocado, pitted and peeled

¼ cup raw cashews *or* ⅓ cup sour cream (dairy or plant-based)

½ teaspoon kosher salt

¼ teaspoon garlic powder

(Ingredients continued on photo)

1. Preheat the air fryer on **BAKE** at 350°F and set the cooking time for 5 minutes. If using a toaster oven–style air fryer, line the cooking pan with aluminum foil.

2. Spread out the chips in a single layer in the air frying basket or on the lined cooking pan. Top each chip with some black beans, olives, a slice of jalapeño, and some cheese.

3. Bake the nachos in the preheated air fryer.

4. **While the nachos are baking, make the crema:** In a blender, combine the avocado oil, water, lime juice, avocado, cashews, salt, and garlic powder. Blend on high speed for 1 minute, until smooth. (Alternatively, you can combine all the crema ingredients in a wide-mouth mason jar and blend with an immersion blender.)

5. Transfer the nachos to a serving plate. Dollop a teaspoon of crema on top of each chip. Top with tomato, cilantro, and onion. Serve right away.

GARNISH

1 Roma or plum tomato, seeded and diced

1 tablespoon chopped fresh cilantro

3 tablespoons minced red onion *or* 1 green onion, thinly sliced

Fried Wontons and Mango "Poke"

It's amazing how much mango tastes just like tuna poke once it's seasoned with sweet soy sauce and mixed with sesame oil, onions, and crunchy macadamia nuts. For a light snack, scoop up the poke with crispy, air-fried wonton chips. For a lunch-worthy bowl, serve the wonton chips on the side and enjoy your "poke" over rice, with shelled edamame, sliced avocado, and a sprinkle of furikake on top.

I large ripe mango, peeled, pitted, and diced

¼ cup chopped sweet onion

1 green onion, finely chopped

2 tablespoons sweet soy sauce (see note)

¼ teaspoon toasted sesame oil

¼ teaspoon gochugaru (Korean red pepper flakes) (optional)

Pinch ground ginger

12 wonton wrappers (plant-based if preferred)

Avocado oil, for spraying

1 tablespoon chopped macadamia nuts, for garnish

NOTE: You can purchase Lee Kum Kee brand sweet soy sauce (or kecap manis) at most Asian grocery stores or online. If you cannot find it, substitute by mixing together 1½ tablespoons regular soy sauce and 1½ teaspoons agave nectar or honey.

1. In a serving bowl, stir together the mango, sweet onion, green onion, sweet soy sauce, sesame oil, gochugaru (if using), and ginger until evenly combined.

2. Preheat the air fryer to **AIR FRY** at 350°F and set the cooking time for 3 minutes.

3. Place 6 wonton wrappers in the air frying basket, then spray them lightly with avocado oil. Turn the wrappers over and spray them on their second sides.

4. Air-fry the wontons in the preheated air fryer. When the **Turn food** notice comes on (or two-thirds of the way through the cooking time), use a pair of tongs to flip the wonton wrappers. It's fine if some of them have folded over.

5. Watch the wonton chips carefully during the second half of cooking—some may take less time than others to cook through. As the chips become golden brown, use tongs to remove from the air fryer and transfer to a serving plate.

6. Repeat the air frying process with the remaining 6 wonton wrappers.

7. Sprinkle the chopped macadamia nuts on top of the poke, and serve with the wonton chips.

Panko Party Wings with Secret Ingredient Katsu Sauce

Panko breadcrumbs make all the difference in these crispy-on-the-outside, juicy-on-the-inside chicken wings. Miso paste lends its umami flavor, and the katsu sauce gets a hit of sweetness and a little kick of spice from gochujang, a Korean red pepper paste. Serve the wings as an afternoon snack or appetizer, with the katsu sauce on the side for dipping or drizzled on top.

WINGS

1 pound chicken party wings (10 to 12)

¼ cup all-purpose flour

1 large egg

1½ tablespoons white miso paste

1½ tablespoons water

1 cup panko breadcrumbs

Avocado oil, for spraying

KATSU SAUCE

2 tablespoons Worcestershire sauce

2 tablespoons ketchup

1 tablespoon gochujang

1 teaspoon soy sauce

1. If using a toaster oven–style air fryer, line the cooking pan with parchment paper.

2. Add the chicken wings to a mixing bowl. Sprinkle them with the flour, then toss to coat evenly.

3. Make a breading station with two shallow bowls. In the first bowl, whisk together the egg, miso paste, and water until thoroughly combined. Add the panko breadcrumbs to the second bowl.

4. Preheat the air fryer on **ROAST** at 350°F and set the cooking time for 20 minutes.

5. Shake any excess flour off one wing, then coat it in the egg wash. Place the wing in the bowl of breadcrumbs and turn it over to lightly coat both sides. Transfer the wing to the lined cooking pan or to a large plate if using a basket-style air fryer. Repeat to bread the remaining wings. Spray the breaded wings lightly with avocado oil.

(Continued)

NOTE: This timing and temperature also work well for nonbreaded wings. I like to season mine with salt and pepper, lemon pepper, or a barbecue rub (page 165). Serve them as is or toss with a little bit of hot sauce.

6. Place the cooking pan in the air fryer, or if using a basket-style air fryer, place the breaded wings in a single layer in the basket. Roast the wings in the preheated air fryer. When the **Turn food** notice comes on (or two-thirds of the way through the cooking time), use a pair of tongs to flip the wings and spray them with avocado oil on their second sides.

7. **While the wings are cooking, make the sauce:** Add the Worcestershire, ketchup, gochujang, and soy sauce to a small bowl and stir to combine. Set aside.

8. When the cooking program ends, transfer the wings to a serving platter. Serve with the katsu on the side for dipping or drizzled on top.

Turkey Monte Cristo Sandwiches

A cross between French toast and grilled cheese, with some deli meat tucked inside, these sandwiches are a savory and sweet lunch that will quickly become a favorite in your house. I like to make mine with turkey, but feel free to use the more traditional sliced ham if you prefer. Serve it on its own, or with a cup of soup alongside.

3 large eggs

1 cup milk

4 tablespoons butter

8 slices sourdough bread or gluten-free bread

2 tablespoons Dijon mustard

Freshly ground black pepper

¼ cup jam (strawberry, raspberry, apricot, peach . . . whatever you like)

4 (1-ounce) slices cheddar, Swiss, or any other semihard/melting cheese

8 (1-ounce) slices deli turkey or ham

Powdered sugar, for serving (optional)

1. If using a toaster oven–style air fryer, line the cooking pan with parchment paper.

2. In a shallow bowl, whisk together the eggs and milk. Set aside.

3. On a cutting board, butter the slices of bread. The buttered sides will be the outsides of your sandwiches. Turn the slices over so their unbuttered sides are facing up, then spread 4 slices with Dijon. Top the mustard with a grind or two of black pepper, then spread the other 4 slices with jam.

4. On top of each mustard-coated slice of bread, add 1 slice of cheese and 2 slices of turkey. Top with the remaining slices of bread, jam side down, to make 4 sandwiches.

5. Preheat the air fryer on **ROAST** at 375°F and set the cooking time for 9 minutes.

6. When the air fryer has preheated, pick up a sandwich with both hands, dunk it into the egg-milk mixture for 5 seconds, turn it over and dunk the second side, then place it on the lined cooking pan or directly in the basket. Repeat with the rest of the sandwiches.

(Continued)

7. Roast the sandwiches in the preheated air fryer.

8. When the **Turn food** notice comes on (or two-thirds of the way through the cooking time), use a thin, flexible spatula to flip the sandwiches.

9. When the cooking program ends, transfer the sandwiches to serving plates, top with a light dusting of powdered sugar (if using), cut in half, and serve right away.

Tempeh Sandwiches with Roasted Garlic Aioli

Use either Tempeh Bacon (page 15) or BBQ Tempeh (page 165) in this hearty, filling, and entirely plant-based sandwich. The homemade vegan aioli features a whole bulb of garlic that's "roasted" in the air fryer.

ROASTED GARLIC

1 head garlic

1½ teaspoons extra-virgin olive oil

¼ teaspoon kosher salt

⅛ teaspoon freshly ground black pepper

AIOLI

⅓ cup extra-virgin olive oil

¼ cup cooked or canned chickpeas or white beans, drained and rinsed

1 tablespoon fresh lemon juice

½ teaspoon kosher salt

SANDWICHES

1 batch Tempeh Bacon (page 15) or BBQ Tempeh (page 165)

8 slices sprouted-grain bread (such as Ezekiel bread)

1 large avocado, pitted, peeled, and sliced

4 romaine lettuce leaves, halved crosswise

2 beefsteak or other slicing tomatoes, thinly sliced

1. Preheat the air fryer on **ROAST** at 375°F and set the cooking time for 20 minutes.

2. Cut off the top ½ inch or so of the head of garlic so that the tops of the garlic cloves are exposed. Place the garlic on an 8-inch square of aluminum foil. Drizzle the olive oil over the garlic, then sprinkle with the salt and pepper. Close up the foil around the garlic. If using a toaster-style air fryer, place it on the cooking pan. If using a basket-style air fryer, place it in the basket.

3. Roast the garlic in the preheated air fryer.

4. When the cooking program ends, remove the garlic and unwrap it from the foil. Let it cool for about 5 minutes, then squeeze out the cloves into a mini blender jar or a wide-mouthed mason jar (if you have an immersion blender).

5. Add the olive oil, chickpeas, lemon juice, and salt to the blender. Blend the aioli for about 1 minute, until it's thickened and smooth. Taste for seasoning, adding more salt if needed.

(Continued)

NOTE: If you like, you can season the sliced avocado and tomato with salt and pepper as you're adding them to the sandwich. A drizzle of olive oil and a sprinkle of red wine vinegar don't hurt either.

6. Cook or rewarm the tempeh. If I'm using leftover tempeh, I use the **BAKE** setting at 300°F for 5 minutes to warm it through.

7. Toast the bread using your air fryer's **TOAST** setting. If your model does not have this setting, use the **BROIL** setting at its highest temperature (some will go up to 450°F, while others top out at 400°F) for 3 to 5 minutes, depending on the level of browning you prefer.

8. Build your sandwiches: Spread a tablespoon of the aioli onto each slice of toast. Top half the slices with avocado, lettuce, tomatoes, and tempeh, then close the sandwiches with the remaining slices of toast. Serve right away.

Dairy-Free, Gluten-Free (if modified), Vegan

PREP TIME: **20 MINUTES (PLUS 30 MINUTES TO MARINATE)**

COOK TIME: **15 MINUTES**

YIELD: **8 ROLLS (2 TO 4 SERVINGS)**

Lemongrass Tofu Rice Paper Rolls with Peanut Sauce

Tofu is marinated in a Vietnamese-inspired, flavor-packed mixture with garlic, shallot, and lots of lemongrass. You can serve it in these refreshing and light rice paper rolls, as written, or look to the recipe note for a heartier sandwich version. It's also yummy atop rice bowls with steamed vegetables—see the chart on page 269 for vegetable cooking times in the Instant Pot.

MARINADE

2 garlic cloves, minced or pressed

1 small shallot, minced, *or*
2 tablespoons minced red onion

2 tablespoons lemongrass paste (see note)

1 tablespoon brown sugar

1 tablespoon avocado oil

1 tablespoon soy sauce or tamari

¼ teaspoon kosher salt

⅛ teaspoon freshly ground black pepper

1 (14-ounce) block extra-firm tofu, cut into ½-inch-thick slices

(Ingredients continued)

1. Combine the garlic, shallot, lemongrass paste, brown sugar, avocado oil, soy sauce, salt, and pepper in a shallow bowl and stir to combine. Add the sliced tofu, turning over the pieces in the marinade so that they are all covered evenly. Marinate for 30 minutes at room temperature, or cover and refrigerate for up to 24 hours.

2. If using a toaster oven–style air fryer, line the cooking pan with parchment. Preheat the air fryer on **BAKE** at 400°F and set the cooking time for 10 minutes.

3. Place the tofu slices on the lined cooking pan, then spoon any leftover marinade on top of them. If using a basket-style air fryer, place the tofu directly in the air frying basket, then spoon the marinade on top.

4. Bake the tofu in the preheated air fryer.

5. When the cooking program ends, set aside the tofu to cool for a few minutes while you make the peanut sauce.

(Continued)

SAUCE

½ cup water

1 tablespoon soy sauce or tamari

¼ teaspoon cornstarch

⅛ teaspoon ground ginger

1½ teaspoons avocado oil

1 garlic clove, minced

¼ cup natural peanut butter

2 tablespoons brown sugar

1 teaspoon sriracha (optional)

ROLLS

8 rice paper wrappers (aka spring roll wrappers)

24 fresh cilantro sprigs, bottom 4 inches cut off

2 cups shredded iceberg lettuce

2 Persian cucumbers, julienned

2 medium carrots, julienned

Sriracha or sambal oelek, for serving

6. **Make the sauce:** In a small bowl, stir together the water, soy sauce, cornstarch, and ginger. In a small saucepan, heat the oil and garlic for about 2 minutes over medium heat, until the garlic is bubbling but not browned. To the pan, add the soy sauce mixture, peanut butter, brown sugar, and sriracha (if using). Stir constantly until the sauce is fully combined, bubbling, and thickened, about 3 minutes. Turn off the heat and set aside.

7. **Make the rolls:** Fill a shallow dish with warm water. Dunk a rice paper wrapper in the warm water, then place it on your work surface. Place 3 cilantro sprigs on the bottom third of the wrapper, then place a (still-warm) slice of tofu on top of the cilantro. Layer ¼ cup of the lettuce, then some of the cucumbers and carrots on top. Tuck in the bottom of the roll, then tuck in the sides. Roll up the spring roll from the bottom, taking care to wrap firmly but not so tightly that you tear the delicate rice paper wrapper. Repeat to make 8 rolls.

8. Serve the rolls with the peanut sauce on the side for dipping, along with extra sriracha if you like more spice. If the peanut sauce has thickened while sitting, add a splash of water and stir until it has reached your desired consistency.

NOTES: This is one of those rare cases where I find that a convenience ingredient works better than its fresh counterpart. Gourmet Garden brand lemongrass paste, available in the produce section of many larger grocery stores, has a finely processed texture and blends well into the tofu marinade, while fresh lemongrass can remain woody and fibrous even when chopped very finely. A 4-ounce tube of the paste will keep for a long time in the fridge.

You can serve the tofu in sandwiches rather than making rice paper rolls, if you like. Spread some mayonnaise on 4 (6-inch-long) sandwich rolls or banh mi (Vietnamese-style) baguettes, then fill each sandwich with 2 slices of tofu and one-quarter of the vegetables listed above. Add a drizzle of sriracha, if you like.

Dairy-Free (if modified),
Gluten-Free (if modified),
Vegan (if modified)

PREP TIME: **15 MINUTES
(PLUS 20 MINUTES FOR
RICE TO COOL)**

COOK TIME: **30 MINUTES**

YIELD: **2 SUSHI ROLLS
(EASILY DOUBLED, SEE
NOTE)**

Sushi Rolls with Basil and Garlic

This is definitely a don't-knock-it-until-you-try-it recipe! The combination of cream cheese, avocado, macadamia nuts, garlic, and basil might sound out of place in a sushi roll, but trust me, these are going to rock your world. They're inspired by one of the rolls at Mobo Sushi in Santa Cruz, where I enjoyed countless vegetarian sushi dinners in my college days. Mobo's version is an inside-out maki, whereas mine has the nori on the outside. It's a little bit easier to roll, no matter your sushi-making skill level, and tastes just as delicious.

¾ cup sushi rice

¾ cup water

**2 tablespoons unseasoned rice
vinegar or white wine vinegar**

1 tablespoon granulated sugar

½ teaspoon kosher salt

1 large garlic clove, minced

2 sheets nori

**4 ounces cream cheese (dairy or
plant-based)**

**½ large avocado, peeled and
sliced**

**¼ cup roasted salted macadamia
nuts, chopped**

8 fresh basil leaves

**2 tablespoons soy sauce or
tamari, for serving**

1. Pour a cup of water into the Instant Pot and place the metal steam rack inside.

2. Add the rice and water to a 1½-quart stainless-steel bowl. Place it on top of the steam rack.

3. Secure the lid and set the pressure release to **Sealing**. Select the **RICE** setting. (The pot will take about 10 minutes to come up to pressure before the cooking program begins.)

4. While the rice cooks, microwave the vinegar, sugar, and salt in a small bowl for 20 seconds, or heat in a small saucepan for 1 to 2 minutes, just until piping hot. Stir to dissolve the sugar and salt, then set aside.

5. Put the minced garlic in a small bowl, cover with boiling water, and let sit for 5 minutes. Drain and set aside.

6. When the cooking program ends, let the pressure release naturally (this will take about 10 minutes).

(Continued)

NOTES: This recipe is easily doubled to 4 rolls. If you are cooking 1½ cups of rice or more, you can add the rice and water directly to the Instant Pot inner pot without using the pot-in-pot method outlined above.

You can use the recipe for sushi rice here, then add whatever fillings you like. Feel free to substitute your own favorite combination of ingredients for the ones used here. Some classic vegetarian maki fillings are cucumber, gobo (pickled burdock), ume (pickled plums), sweetened shiitake mushrooms, tamago (sweetened omelet), and shiso leaves. Tempura green beans or sticks of tempura sweet potato would also be great substitutes.

7. Wearing heat-resistant mitts, remove the bowl of rice from the Instant Pot. Pour the vinegar mixture over the rice and stir. Let the rice cool for about 20 minutes, stirring it every few minutes, until it's just a little bit warm.

8. Place a nori sheet on a sushi mat, shiny side down.

9. Wet your hands to keep the rice from sticking, then spread half of the rice on the nori sheet, leaving a bare 1-inch strip of nori at the end farthest from you.

10. In the middle of the rice, use your fingers to make a horizontal line with half the cream cheese. Top the line of cream cheese with half of the avocado slices, half of the macadamia nuts, half of the drained garlic, and half of the basil leaves.

11. Dab some water on the inch of exposed nori. Roll up the sushi from the bottom of the roll, securely tucking in the filling, then continue to roll until it is a complete cylinder. Let it rest for a minute inside the sushi mat, then unroll the mat and place the sushi roll on a cutting board, seam side down.

12. Repeat to make second roll.

13. With a very sharp knife, cut each roll into 8 slices, rinsing the knife between slices for a clean result.

14. Serve the rolls with soy sauce alongside for dipping. They're very flavorful and a little soy goes a long way—you'll just want a dab.

Dairy-Free, Gluten-Free (if modified), Vegetarian

PREP TIME: **10 MINUTES**   COOK TIME: **5 MINUTES**   YIELD: **4 OPEN-FACED SANDWICHES**

Avocado Egg Salad Sandwiches

These mean, green egg salad sandwiches are extra nutritious thanks to the addition of mashed avocado. I like to enjoy mine open-faced, with cherry tomatoes and sliced red onion on top. You can also serve the egg salad in a bowl with crackers alongside for an easy snack.

EGG SALAD

3 hard-boiled eggs (page 13)

1 large avocado, pitted and peeled

1 tablespoon mayonnaise

1½ teaspoons fresh lemon juice

¼ teaspoon kosher salt

⅛ teaspoon freshly ground black pepper

SANDWICHES

4 thick slices crusty artisan bread, such as a boule or bâtard, *or* gluten-free bread

2 tablespoons mayonnaise

2 teaspoons yellow mustard

4 iceberg, green leaf, butter, or romaine lettuce leaves

⅓ cup cherry tomatoes, halved

¼ cup thinly sliced red onion

Everything bagel seasoning, za'atar, or toasted sesame seeds

Freshly ground black pepper

Flaky salt

1. Peel the hard-boiled eggs. Cut the eggs in half, then pop out the yolks into a mixing bowl.

2. To the bowl with the egg yolks, add the avocado, mayonnaise, lemon juice, salt, and pepper. Use a fork to mash the mixture until fairly smooth. Chop up the egg whites, then stir them in. Taste for seasoning, adding more salt if needed.

3. Toast the bread using your air fryer's **TOAST** setting. If your model does not have this setting, use the **BROIL** setting at its highest temperature (some will go up to 450°F, while others top out at 400°F) for 3 to 5 minutes, depending on the level of browning you prefer.

4. Spread a thin layer of mayonnaise and mustard on each slice of toast. Top each slice with a lettuce leaf, ¼ cup of the egg salad, a sprinkle of cherry tomatoes, and a few slices of red onion. Sprinkle on your choice of seasoning, along with a grind or two of pepper and a sprinkle of flaky salt. Serve right away.

Potato and Tuna Salad with Shallots and Capers

Potato salad usually serves as a side dish, but when you add a couple cans of tuna, it becomes a whole meal on its own. The potatoes steam quickly in the Instant Pot while you put together a warm vinaigrette, and you can enjoy the salad warm, at room temperature, or chilled. Add a few lettuce leaves alongside for making wraps, or place them on the plate and pile your potato salad on top.

1½ **pounds petite/baby gold potatoes (halved if larger than 1½ inches in diameter)**

3 tablespoons extra-virgin olive oil

2 shallots, sliced into ⅛-inch-thick rounds

2 tablespoons capers, drained and rinsed

3 tablespoons apple cider vinegar

2 teaspoons Dijon mustard

½ teaspoon freshly ground black pepper

¼ teaspoon kosher salt

2 (5-ounce) cans skipjack tuna (water- or oil-packed), drained

½ cup chopped fresh flat-leaf parsley

Leaves from 1 head butter or romaine lettuce, for serving

1. Pour a cup of water into the Instant Pot and place the steamer basket inside. Add the potatoes to the steamer basket.

2. Secure the lid and set the pressure release to **Sealing**. Select the **PRESSURE COOK** or **MANUAL** setting for 4 minutes at high pressure. (The pot will take about 10 minutes to come up to pressure before the cooking program begins.)

3. **While the potatoes are cooking, make the warm dressing:** In a small skillet on the stove, heat the olive oil and shallots over medium heat. Sauté until the shallots are softened and just beginning to brown, about 4 minutes. Turn off the heat, then stir in the capers, vinegar, mustard, pepper, and salt. Set aside.

4. When the cooking program ends, perform a quick pressure release by moving the pressure release to **Venting**. Open the pot. Transfer the potatoes to a cutting board. While they're still warm, cut them into slices or quarters.

(Continued)

5. Add the potatoes to a mixing bowl, along with the warm dressing, tuna, and parsley. Stir to combine, breaking up the tuna a bit so it mixes into the salad. Taste for seasoning, adding more salt if needed.

6. Serve warm or chilled, with lettuce leaves.

Personal Pesto Pizzas

Each person gets their own pizza, topped with a flavorful pesto, mozzarella cheese, and a handful of halved cherry tomatoes. Use the recipes for pesto and pizza dough given here, or go for a super-quick version and use ¾ cup store-bought pesto and 1 pound store-bought pizza dough. I make these pizzas as free-form ovals rather than tidy circles—kids can have some fun helping with this step, as perfection is not the goal!

DOUGH

2 cups all-purpose flour, plus more for dusting

¾ cup warm water

1 teaspoon kosher salt

1 teaspoon instant yeast

PESTO

1 large bunch basil, stems removed

¼ cup walnut pieces

¼ cup grated parmesan cheese

1 garlic clove, chopped

½ teaspoon kosher salt

¼ teaspoon freshly ground black pepper

¼ cup extra-virgin olive oil

1. **Make the dough:** Combine the flour, water, salt, and yeast in a 6-cup storage container or a 1½- to 2-quart bowl that will fit in your air fryer. Use a dough whisk or your hands to combine the ingredients into a shaggy dough, kneading for about 2 minutes until the dough comes away from the sides of the container.

2. Cover the container tightly with a reusable lid or plastic wrap and place it in the air fryer. Select the **PROOF** or **DEHYDRATE** setting for 40 minutes at 95°F.

3. **While the dough is proofing in the air fryer, make the pesto:** Combine the basil leaves, walnuts, parmesan, garlic, salt, pepper, and olive oil in a food processor in the order listed. Process in 10 pulses, scraping down the sides of the processor as needed, until you have a fairly coarse pesto.

4. **Make the flatbreads:** If using a toaster oven–style air fryer, line the cooking pan with parchment paper. Flour a work surface.

(Continued)

TOPPINGS

1 cup shredded Italian cheese blend

½ cup cherry tomatoes, sliced

FOR SERVING

Grated parmesan cheese

Red pepper flakes

5. Transfer the risen dough to the work surface and divide it into 4 pieces. Shape each piece into a 5 × 7-inch oval.

6. Select the **BAKE** setting for 8 minutes at 400°F.

7. When the oven has preheated, place 2 of the dough ovals on the lined cooking pan or in the air frying basket. Top each with 3 tablespoons pesto, ¼ cup shredded cheese, and a sprinkle of cherry tomatoes. (If using a basket-style air fryer, wear heat-resistant mitts while doing this step.)

8. Bake the pizzas in the preheated air fryer.

9. Transfer the cooked pizzas to a cutting board.

10. Again select the **BAKE** setting for 8 minutes at 400°F, then top and bake the remaining 2 pizzas.

11. Cut the pizzas into wedges and serve, with parmesan and red pepper flakes at the table.

Dairy-Free (if modified),
Gluten-Free (if modified),
Vegan (if modified),
Vegetarian

PREP TIME: **5 MINUTES**   COOK TIME: **9 MINUTES**   YIELD: **1 QUESADILLA (2 SERVINGS)**

Veggie and Black Bean Quesadilla

One hearty whole-wheat quesadilla is plenty to serve two people as an afternoon snack. When you make them in the air fryer, there's no flipping required to get crispy, browned tortillas, top and bottom. This one is fairly light on the cheese, with just enough to hold together a nutritious and colorful filling of beans and vegetables. Add another ¼ cup cheese if you want a more ooey-gooey quesadilla.

½ cup shredded Mexican cheese blend, Monterey Jack, or cheddar (dairy or plant-based)

¼ cup diced yellow onion

¼ cup diced bell pepper (any color)

¼ cup fresh or thawed frozen corn kernels

¼ cup cooked or canned black beans, drained and rinsed

1 tablespoon chopped fresh cilantro

¼ teaspoon chili powder

1½ teaspoons unsalted butter (dairy or plant-based)

2 (10-inch) whole-wheat tortillas or gluten-free tortillas (such as Siete)

Salsa (your favorite store-bought or homemade variety), for serving

Sour cream, for serving

1. In a bowl, stir together the cheese, onion, bell pepper, corn, black beans, cilantro, and chili powder until evenly mixed.

2. Preheat the air fryer on **BAKE** at 350°F and set the cooking time for 9 minutes. If using a toaster oven–style air fryer, line the cooking pan with parchment paper.

3. Spread half of the butter evenly over one side of one tortilla, then place it, butter side down, on the lined cooking pan. Spread the filling mixture evenly over the tortilla. Butter one side of the remaining tortilla and place it on top of the filling, butter side up.

4. Place the lined cooking pan with the quesadilla in the air fryer, or place the quesadilla directly in the air frying basket. Bake the quesadilla in the preheated air fryer.

5. When the cooking program ends, slide the quesadilla out onto a cutting board and cut it into wedges. Serve right away, with salsa and sour cream on the side.

CHAPTER 3

SOUPS & TOPPERS

Dairy-Free (if modified),
Gluten-Free (if modified),
Vegan (if modified)

PREP TIME: **5 MINUTES**　　　COOK TIME: **35 MINUTES**　　　YIELD: **4 TO 6 SERVINGS**

Classic Tomato Soup

A bowl of piping-hot tomato soup is one of my favorite lunches on cold winter days, especially when paired with Grilled Cheese Dippers (page 79). Garlic, onions, carrots, and celery add depth of flavor. This classic sipper is creamy and smooth even without the (optional) cream, thanks to the addition of a handful of rice that gets blended in at the end of cooking.

2 tablespoons extra-virgin olive oil or butter

2 garlic cloves, minced

1 yellow onion, diced

2 carrots, peeled and diced

2 celery stalks, diced

1 teaspoon kosher salt

1½ teaspoons Italian seasoning

2 cups low-sodium vegetable broth

¼ cup uncooked white rice or quick-cooking brown rice

1 (28-ounce) can whole peeled tomatoes and their liquid

¼ cup heavy cream or half-and-half (optional)

Freshly ground black pepper, for serving

Grilled Cheese Dippers (page 79) or Croutons Two Ways (page 80), for serving (optional)

1. Select the **SAUTÉ** setting on the Instant Pot and heat the olive oil and garlic. When the garlic begins to bubble, add the onion, carrots, celery, and salt. Sauté for about 5 minutes, until the vegetables are beginning to soften. Add the Italian seasoning and sauté for another 30 seconds or so, until aromatic.

2. Add the broth, rice, and tomatoes and their liquid, breaking up the tomatoes with your hands as you add them. Stir to combine.

3. Secure the lid and set the pressure release to **Sealing**. Press **Cancel** to reset the cooking program, then select the **PRESSURE COOK** or **MANUAL** setting for 10 minutes at high pressure. (The pot will take about 10 minutes to come up to pressure before the cooking program begins.)

4. When the cooking program ends, let the pressure release naturally for at least 10 minutes, then move the pressure release to **Venting** to release any remaining steam. Open the pot, add the cream (if using), and use an immersion blender to puree the soup until smooth. Taste for seasoning, adding more salt if needed.

5. Ladle the soup into serving bowls. Top with a grind or two of black pepper and serve right away, with grilled cheese dippers or croutons, if you like.

Dairy-Free, Gluten-Free, Vegan　　PREP TIME: **5 MINUTES**　　COOK TIME: **25 MINUTES**　　YIELD: **4 TO 6 SERVINGS**

Peanut, Sweet Potato, and Tomato Soup

I love a fast recipe that tastes like it took a long time to prepare, don't you? Thanks to flavorful ingredients like curry powder, fire-roasted diced tomatoes, and peanut butter, this African-inspired soup turns out so much tastier than its relatively short ingredient list and prep time would lead you to believe. While it cooks under pressure, make a topping of Coconut, Peanut, and Sesame Crunch (page 83) to sprinkle on top, or go the easy route and sprinkle on some roasted salted peanuts instead. The soup can be served on its own or over rice—look to the recipe note on page 62 for a pot-in-pot option to cook rice at the same time.

1 tablespoon extra-virgin olive oil

1-inch piece ginger, peeled and minced

4 garlic cloves, minced or pressed

1 medium red onion, diced

1½ teaspoons curry powder

1 teaspoon kosher salt

2 cups low-sodium vegetable broth

1 pound orange sweet potatoes (aka garnet yams), peeled and cut into ½-inch dice

1 (14.5-ounce) can fire-roasted diced tomatoes and their liquid

1 tablespoon tomato paste

½ cup natural creamy peanut butter

1. Select the **SAUTÉ** setting on the Instant Pot and heat the olive oil, ginger, and garlic for 2 minutes, until the garlic is bubbling but not browned. Add the onion and sauté for 3 minutes, until it begins to soften. Add the curry powder, salt, and broth, using a wooden spoon to nudge any browned bits from the bottom of the pot.

2. Add the sweet potatoes and stir to combine. Add the diced tomatoes and tomato paste on top, but do not stir them in.

3. Secure the lid and set the pressure release to **Sealing**. Press the **Cancel** button to reset the cooking program, then select the **PRESSURE COOK** or **MANUAL** setting for 1 minute at high pressure. (The pot will take about 10 minutes to come up to pressure before the cooking program begins.)

4. When the cooking program ends, let the pressure release naturally for at least 10 minutes, then move the pressure release to **Venting** to release any remaining steam. Open the pot, add the peanut butter, and stir to combine.

(Continued)

FOR SERVING

Coconut, Peanut, and Sesame Crunch (page 83) *or* 1 cup roasted salted peanuts

Fresh cilantro sprigs

3 cups cooked rice (optional; see note)

5. Ladle the soup into serving bowls. Garnish with the crunchy topping and cilantro and serve right away, with rice alongside, if you like.

NOTE: If you'd like, you can cook a bowl of rice right on top of the soup using the pot-in-pot technique. Add a raised metal steam rack to the pot after you've added the diced tomatoes and tomato paste to the soup. Place a 1½-quart stainless-steel bowl on the rack, and add 1 cup long-grain white rice, 1 cup water, and ¼ teaspoon kosher salt to the bowl. Increase the cooking time to 10 minutes at high pressure. The sweet potatoes will break down into the soup with this longer cooking time, giving it a thicker texture.

Dairy-Free (if modified),
Gluten-Free (if modified),
Vegan (if modified)

PREP TIME: **5 MINUTES**   COOK TIME: **40 MINUTES**   YIELD: **4 SERVINGS**

Roasted Red Pepper and Onion Bisque

I love to make soups that start with roasted vegetables, as this extra step concentrates and caramelized the flavors. When you use an air fryer to roast veggies, the preheat and cook times are cut in at least half compared with a traditional oven. Red peppers and onions become extra sweet and well browned around the edges, and all that flavor goes into this creamy yet light soup. Serve it with garlic-herb or smoked paprika croutons (page 80) for crunchy contrast or with Turkey Monte Cristo Sandwiches (page 37) for a heartier meal.

2 large red bell peppers, seeded and diced

1 medium yellow onion, diced

2 garlic cloves, pressed or minced

1 tablespoon extra-virgin olive oil

½ teaspoon kosher salt

1 (14-ounce) can diced tomatoes and their liquid

8 ounces Yukon Gold potatoes, diced

2 cups low-sodium vegetable broth

1 teaspoon dried oregano

¼ cup half-and-half (dairy or plant-based)

Croutons Two Ways (page 80), for serving (optional)

1. Preheat the air fryer on **ROAST** at 375°F and set the cooking time for 15 minutes. If using a toaster oven–style air fryer, line the cooking pan with parchment paper.

2. In a large bowl, toss together the bell peppers, onion, garlic, olive oil, and salt.

3. Spread out the vegetables in an even layer on the cooking pan. If using a basket-style air fryer, add the vegetables directly to the basket.

4. Roast the vegetables in the preheated air fryer.

5. While the vegetables are roasting, in the Instant Pot, combine the tomatoes, potatoes, vegetable broth, and oregano.

6. When the vegetables finish roasting, add them to the Instant Pot.

(Continued)

7. Secure the Instant Pot lid and set the pressure release to **Sealing**. Select the **PRESSURE COOK** or **MANUAL** setting for 3 minutes at high pressure. (The pot will take about 10 minutes to come up to pressure before the cooking program begins.)

8. When the cooking program ends, let the pressure release naturally for at least 10 minutes, then move the pressure release to **Venting** to release any remaining steam.

9. Open the pot. Add the half-and-half and use an immersion blender or a regular blender to puree the soup until smooth. Taste for seasoning and add salt if needed.

10. Ladle the soup into serving bowls. Serve hot, with croutons on top or alongside, if you like.

White Bean and Potato Soup

This hearty, chunky soup features lots and lots of white beans and vegetables in a thick, tomatoey broth. Serve it topped with smoked paprika croutons (page 80), or with slices of crusty artisan bread, for a rustic and tasty meal.

3 tablespoons extra-virgin olive oil, plus more for serving

1 small yellow onion, diced

1 carrot, peeled and diced

2 celery stalks, diced

½ teaspoon kosher salt

1½ teaspoons chopped fresh rosemary *or* 1 teaspoon dried

1 bay leaf

2 cups low-sodium vegetable broth

8 ounces russet or Yukon Gold potatoes, peeled and diced

2 (15-ounce) cans Great Northern beans, drained and rinsed, *or* 3 cups cooked beans (from 8 ounces dried)

¾ cup (½ [14-ounce] can) petite diced tomatoes and their liquid *or* 2 Roma or plum tomatoes, diced

¼ cup tomato paste

Smoked paprika croutons (page 80) or crusty bread, for serving (optional)

1. Select the **SAUTÉ** setting on the Instant Pot and heat the olive oil for about 2 minutes, until shimmering. Add the onion, carrot, celery, and salt and sauté for about 3 minutes, until the onions are beginning to soften. Add the rosemary and bay leaf and sauté for 1 more minute.

2. Stir in the broth, potatoes, and beans. Add the tomatoes and tomato paste on top, but do not stir.

3. Secure the lid and set the pressure release to **Sealing**. Select the **PRESSURE COOK** or **MANUAL** setting for 5 minutes at high pressure. (The pot will take about 10 minutes to come up to pressure before the cooking program begins.)

4. When the cooking program ends, let the pressure release naturally for at least 10 minutes, then move the pressure release to **Venting** to release any remaining steam.

5. Open the pot and stir the soup. Remove and discard the bay leaf. Taste for seasoning, adding more salt if needed.

6. Ladle the soup into serving bowls, drizzle with olive oil, sprinkle with croutons, if you like, and serve right away.

Dairy-Free (if modified), Gluten-Free (if modified), Vegan (if modified), Vegetarian

PREP TIME: **5 MINUTES**   COOK TIME: **55 MINUTES**   YIELD: **4 TO 6 SERVINGS**

Pantry Vegetable and Barley Soup

I like to have recipes in my back pocket that only require ingredients I am guaranteed to have on hand in my kitchen, and this soup is one of them. It's so simple and yet so good, a classically comforting veggie soup with grains of chewy barley throughout. Serve it with Parmesan and Rosemary Crisps (page 84), or with a sprinkle of store-bought plant-based parm for an entirely plant-based meal.

2 tablespoons extra-virgin olive oil

1 yellow onion, diced

2 celery stalks, diced

1 teaspoon Italian seasoning

1 teaspoon kosher salt

4 cups low-sodium vegetable broth

1 (1-pound) bag frozen mixed vegetables

1 (15-ounce) can petite diced tomatoes and their liquid

½ cup pearl barley

Parmesan and Rosemary Crisps (page 84), for serving (optional)

NOTE: To make the soup gluten-free, substitute medium-grain brown rice for the barley.

1. Select the **SAUTÉ** setting on the Instant Pot and heat the olive oil for 2 minutes. Add the onion, celery, Italian seasoning, and salt and sauté for about 4 more minutes, until the onion is softened.

2. Stir in the broth, frozen mixed vegetables, tomatoes, and barley.

3. Secure the lid and set the pressure release to **Sealing**. Press the **Cancel** button to reset the cooking program, then select the **PRESSURE COOK** or **MANUAL** setting for 20 minutes at high pressure. (The pot will take about 15 minutes to come up to pressure before the cooking program begins.)

4. When the cooking program ends, let the pressure release for at least 15 minutes, then move the pressure release to **Venting** to release any remaining steam. Open the pot. Taste for seasoning, adding salt if needed.

5. Ladle the soup into bowls and serve with the parmesan crisps, if you like.

Lemony Farro and Chicken Soup

This soup is inspired by Greek avgolemono, with its lemony broth made creamy thanks to the addition of egg yolks. Farro, a nutritious and filling whole-grain form of wheat, takes the place of the usual rice or orzo pasta. It makes the soup just hearty enough to enjoy on its own as a light meal. For bigger appetites, round out the meal with a side of Tzatziki Dip (page 153) and pita bread triangles.

1 pound boneless, skinless chicken breasts or tenders

4 cups low-sodium chicken broth

½ cup pearled or quick-cooking farro

1 teaspoon dried oregano

½ teaspoon kosher salt

¼ teaspoon freshly ground black pepper

¼ cup fresh lemon juice

2 large egg yolks

1 tablespoon chopped fresh dill and/or flat-leaf parsley, for serving

Extra-virgin olive oil, for serving

1. Add the chicken, broth, farro, oregano, salt, and pepper to the Instant Pot.

2. Secure the lid in the **Sealing** position. Select the **PRESSURE COOK** or **MANUAL** setting for 15 minutes at high pressure. (It will take about 15 minutes to come up to pressure before the cooking program begins.)

3. When the cooking program ends, let the pressure release naturally for 10 minutes, then move the pressure release to **Venting** to release the steam.

4. Use a pair of tongs to transfer the chicken to a dish, then use two forks to shred the chicken.

5. Transfer 1 cup of broth from the pot to a bowl, then whisk in the lemon juice and egg yolks.

(Continued)

6. Return the lemon-broth mixture and the shredded chicken to the pot and stir to combine. Press **Cancel** to reset the cooking program, then select the **SAUTÉ** setting. Let the mixture come up to a simmer and thicken, stirring occasionally, about 5 minutes, then turn off the pot. Taste for seasoning, adding salt if needed.

7. Ladle the soup into bowls. Serve topped with the dill and a generous drizzle of olive oil.

Tofu or Chicken Taco Soup

Whether I make this taco soup with tofu or chicken, it's my go-to dinner when we want something Mexican-inspired that's lighter than a chili and faster than a pozole. Packed with diced tomatoes, black beans, mild green chiles, and corn, it's a colorful and nutritious soup. Make sure to serve it with all of the toppings, including Crispy Tortilla Strips (page 87) or store-bought tortilla chips for a satisfying crunch.

SOUP

2 tablespoons extra-virgin olive oil

2 garlic cloves, minced

1 medium yellow onion, diced

1 tablespoon chili powder

1 teaspoon ground cumin

1 teaspoon ground coriander

½ teaspoon kosher salt

3 cups low-sodium vegetable or chicken broth

1 (15-ounce) can petite diced tomatoes and their liquid

1 (15-ounce) can black beans, drained and rinsed

1 (7-ounce) can diced green chiles

1¼ cups fresh or frozen corn kernels

1 (14-ounce) block extra-firm tofu, cut into ½-inch cubes, *or* 1 pound boneless, skinless chicken breasts, cut into 2-inch pieces

1. Select the **SAUTÉ** setting on the Instant Pot and heat the olive oil and garlic for about 2 minutes, until the garlic is bubbling and golden. Add the onion and sauté for about 3 more minutes, until it is beginning to soften. Add the chili powder, cumin, coriander, and salt and sauté for another 30 seconds or so.

2. Add the broth, tomatoes, beans, chiles, and corn. Stir to combine, using a wooden spoon to nudge any browned bits from the bottom of the pot. Add the pieces of tofu or chicken on top, but do not stir them in.

3. Secure the lid and set the pressure release to **Sealing**. Press the **Cancel** button to reset the cooking program, then select the **PRESSURE COOK** or **MANUAL** setting for 5 minutes at high pressure if using tofu or 15 minutes at high pressure if using chicken. (The pot will take about 15 minutes to come up to pressure before the cooking program begins.)

(Continued)

TOPPINGS

¾ cup sour cream (dairy or plant-based)

½ cup chopped fresh cilantro

½ cup diced red or white onion

Crispy Tortilla Strips (page 87)

1 lime, cut into 6 wedges

Hot sauce (such as Cholula or Tapatío)

NOTE: While the soup is cooking, you can make the Crispy Tortilla Strips (page 87).

4. When the cooking program ends, let the pressure naturally release for at least 15 minutes, then move the pressure release to **Venting** to release any remaining steam.

5. Open the pot. If you used tofu, just stir the soup to mix it in. If you used chicken, use tongs to transfer the chicken to a dish, use two forks to shred the meat, then return it to pot and stir to combine.

6. Ladle the soup into bowls and serve it topped with the sour cream, cilantro, onion, and tortilla strips, with lime wedges and hot sauce on the side.

Dairy-Free (if modified), Gluten-Free (if modified)   PREP TIME: **5 MINUTES**   COOK TIME: **40 MINUTES**   YIELD: **4 TO 6 SERVINGS**

Ground Beef and Cabbage Soup

The first time I had this Eastern European–style soup at Max's Opera Cafe in San Francisco, I knew I wanted to make my own version at home. I make it with ground beef and cabbage in a fairly light sweet-and-sour broth. Serve it with some crusty rye bread and pickles on the side for a great cold weather meal.

1 tablespoon extra-virgin olive oil

1 pound ground beef (90% or leaner)

1 yellow onion, diced

2 carrots, peeled and sliced into ¼-inch rounds

½ teaspoon kosher salt

½ teaspoon freshly ground black pepper

3 cups low-sodium beef or vegetable broth

¼ cup golden raisins

2 tablespoons brown sugar

2 tablespoons white wine vinegar

1 bay leaf

1 pound green cabbage (½ medium head), cored and cut into 1-inch square pieces

1 (8-ounce) can no-salt-added tomato sauce

(Ingredients continued on photo)

1. Select the **SAUTÉ** setting on the Instant Pot and heat the olive oil. Add the ground beef and sauté for 5 minutes, breaking it up with a spatula, until it is cooked through and no traces of pink remain. Add the onion, carrots, salt, and pepper and sauté for 3 minutes, until the onion is beginning to soften.

2. Add the broth, raisins, brown sugar, vinegar, and bay leaf and stir to combine. Sprinkle in the cabbage in an even layer, then pour the tomato sauce on top, but do not stir.

3. Secure the lid and set the pressure release to **Sealing**. Press the **Cancel** button to reset the cooking program, then select the **PRESSURE COOK** or **MANUAL** setting for 5 minutes at high pressure. (It will take about 10 minutes for the pot to come up to pressure before the cooking program begins.)

4. Let the pressure release naturally for at least 15 minutes, then move the pressure release to **Venting** to release any remaining steam. Open the pot and stir the soup. Remove and discard the bay leaf.

5. Ladle the soup into bowls and serve piping hot, with a dollop of sour cream (if using) and parsley sprinkled on top. Offer rye bread and pickles on the side.

FOR SERVING

Sour cream, crème fraîche,
or whole-milk yogurt (dairy or plant-
based; optional)

Chopped fresh flat-leaf parsley

Rye bread or gluten-free bread

Dill pickles

Dairy-Free (if modified),
Gluten-Free (if modified),
Vegan (if modified),
Vegetarian

PREP TIME: **5 MINUTES**   COOK TIME: **7 MINUTES**   YIELD: **4 SERVINGS**

Grilled Cheese Dippers

This is your basic and wonderful grilled cheese in all of its melty, toasty glory. After air frying, the sandwiches are sliced into strips that are perfect for dunking into Classic Tomato Soup (page 59). Use whatever melting cheese you prefer—sharp cheddar is my favorite, but Muenster, provolone, fontina, and American are excellent choices, too.

2 tablespoons butter (dairy or plant-based) or mayonnaise

4 slices sourdough, whole-wheat, multigrain, or gluten-free sandwich bread

2 (1-ounce) slices cheddar or other melting cheese (dairy or plant-based)

2 tablespoons shredded or grated parmesan (optional)

NOTE: To make extra-gooey and -cheesy sandwiches, double the cheese.

1. Preheat the air fryer on **BAKE** at 375°F and set cooking time for 7 minutes. If using a toaster oven–style air fryer, line the cooking pan with parchment paper.

2. Spread the butter or mayonnaise on one side of each slice of bread. Place the bread, buttered side down, on a plate or on the lined cooking pan.

3. Place a slice of cheese on 2 pieces of bread. Top with the remaining bread, buttered side up. Sprinkle the parmesan (if using) evenly over the top of each sandwich.

4. Place the cooking pan in the air fryer, or if using a basket-style air fryer, place the sandwiches in the basket. Bake the sandwiches in the preheated air fryer.

5. When the cooking program ends, transfer the sandwiches to a cutting board and cut them into 1-inch-wide strips. Serve right away, with soup alongside for dunking.

Dairy-Free (if modified),
Gluten-Free (if modified),
Vegan (if modified),
Vegetarian

PREP TIME: **5 MINUTES**   COOK TIME: **9 MINUTES**   YIELD: **ABOUT 2 CUPS**

Croutons Two Ways

When I make soup in the Instant Pot, I usually want something crunchy to add on top or alongside. Enter the air fryer, which makes these buttery croutons come out extra crispy and evenly browned. You can flavor them any way you like. I've included my two favorite variations here, a smoky paprika version as well as one with Italian herbs and garlic. Sprinkle croutons on top of Roasted Red Pepper and Onion Bisque (page 63), White Bean and Potato Soup (page 66), Classic Tomato Soup (page 59), or a salad.

2 slices sourdough, French, or gluten-free bread, cut into ½- to ¾-inch cubes

2 tablespoons unsalted butter (dairy or plant-based), melted

SPICE BLEND

¼ teaspoon smoked paprika

⅛ teaspoon ground coriander

⅛ teaspoon ground cumin

or

½ teaspoon garlic powder

½ teaspoon Italian seasoning

NOTE: If you prefer your croutons a little soft in the middle (as opposed to crunchy all the way through), reduce the cooking time to 6 minutes. You'll want to use them right away, as they won't keep as well as crunchier croutons.

1. Preheat the air fryer on **BAKE** at 350°F and set the cooking time for 9 minutes. If using a toaster oven–style air fryer, line the cooking pan with parchment paper.

2. Place the bread cubes in a mixing bowl. Drizzle the melted butter over the bread and toss to combine. Sprinkle in your preferred spice mix and toss once more, until the cubes of bread are evenly coated.

3. Spread out the bread on the lined cooking pan in a single layer, or directly in the air frying basket if using a basket-style air fryer. Bake the croutons in the preheated air fryer.

4. When the **Turn food** notice comes on (or two-thirds of the way through the cooking time), stir or shake the croutons.

5. Use the croutons right away, or let them cool to room temperature, about 20 minutes, then store in a tightly lidded container for up to 1 week.

Coconut, Peanut, and Sesame Crunch

Peanut, Sweet Potato, and Tomato Soup (page 60) gets a wonderfully crunchy topping that takes just a few minutes to put together. Flakes of coconut, peanuts, and sesame seeds are coated in a sweet and spicy mixture, made golden with a pinch of turmeric. I make this in the air fryer while the soup is cooking, so everything is done at the same time.

½ cup unsweetened flaked coconut (I use Trader Joe's unsweetened coconut chips)

½ cup roasted salted peanuts

2 tablespoons sesame seeds (white, black, toasted, or a mixture)

1 tablespoon agave nectar

1 tablespoon avocado oil

¼ teaspoon ground turmeric

¼ teaspoon red pepper flakes (optional)

¼ teaspoon kosher salt

1. Preheat the air fryer on **BAKE** at 300°F and set the cooking time for 10 minutes. If using a toaster oven–style air fryer, line the cooking pan with parchment paper. If using a basket-style air fryer, cut a 12-inch square of aluminum foil. Press the foil down into the air frying basket, making sure it goes only a couple inches up the sides. Trim if necessary, then remove the foil from the air fryer (you don't want it in there during the preheating, as it won't be weighed down).

2. In a bowl, stir together the coconut, peanuts, sesame seeds, agave nectar, avocado oil, turmeric, red pepper flakes (if using), and salt until evenly combined.

3. If using a toaster oven–style air fryer, spread out the mixture in an even layer on the lined cooking pan. If using a basket-style air fryer, place the foil in the basket, then add the mixture and spread it out in an even layer.

4. Bake the crunch topping in the preheated air fryer.

5. Let the crunch topping cool on the cooking pan or in the air frying basket for at least 10 minutes, then break it up and serve over soup. To store any leftover crunch, let it cool to room temperature, then transfer to a tightly lidded container and store at room temperature for up to 2 weeks.

Parmesan and Rosemary Crisps

Called frico in Italian, these cracker-like disks are made completely out of cheese. I like to season mine with a bit of fresh rosemary and black pepper, then serve them on top of my Pantry Vegetable and Barley Soup (page 69). Look to the recipe note below for directions to make these in a basket-style air fryer.

9 tablespoons shredded parmesan cheese

1 teaspoon chopped fresh rosemary

Freshly ground black pepper

NOTE: A basket-style air fryer is not ideal for making these crisps with the recipe as written, as the cheese will tend to blow around too much if cooked directly in a lined air frying basket. You can use silicone muffin cups, however. Spoon 1 tablespoon cheese into each of 9 silicone muffin cups, top each pile of cheese with the rosemary and black pepper, and bake in the preheated air fryer as instructed here. Allow the crisps to cool in the muffin cups for 15 minutes before unmolding.

1. Preheat a toaster oven–style air fryer on **BAKE** at 350°F and set the cooking time for 3 minutes. Line the cooking pan with parchment paper.

2. Spoon the parmesan cheese onto the parchment in 1-tablespoon piles, about an inch apart. Top each pile with a little pinch of rosemary, then a small grind of black pepper. Use your fingers to flatten the piles just a little bit—don't spread them out too much.

3. Bake the crisps in the preheated air fryer.

4. When the cooking program ends, let the crisps sit in the air fryer for another 2 minutes, then remove them from the air fryer and let cool to room temperature right on the cooking pan, about 15 minutes.

5. Serve the crisps alongside or on top of soup.

Crispy Tortilla Strips

Corn tortillas are sliced into strips, seasoned simply with chili powder, then air-fried until they are just as crispy as a deep-fried tortilla chip, without all the extra oil. Serve them over Tofu or Chicken Taco Soup (page 73) or Tempeh or Beef Chili (page 111)—if you can keep from snacking on them all first.

4 (6-inch) corn tortillas, cut into ½ × 2-inch strips

1 tablespoon extra-virgin olive oil

¾ teaspoon chili powder

¼ teaspoon kosher salt

1. Preheat the air fryer on **AIR FRY** at 300°F and set the cooking time for 15 minutes.

2. In a mixing bowl, toss the tortilla strips with the olive oil, chili powder, and salt.

3. Spread out the tortilla strips in an even layer in the air frying basket.

4. Air fry the tortilla strips. When the **Turn food** notice comes on (or two-thirds of the way through the cooking time), shake the tortilla strips.

5. When the program ends, remove the basket from the oven and let the strips cool for about 5 minutes, until they're no longer sizzling hot but still nice and warm. Serve sprinkled on top of soup.

CHAPTER 4

STEWS & CHILIS

Dairy-Free (if modified), Gluten-Free, Vegan (if modified), Vegetarian

PREP TIME: **5 MINUTES (PLUS 15 MINUTES TO SIT)**

COOK TIME: **15 MINUTES**

YIELD: **4 SERVINGS**

Eggplant Chickpea Stew with Mint and Feta

Eggplant becomes silky and tender when cooked under pressure—it practically falls apart and mixes with the tomato-based broth to provide a rich and saucy background for tender chickpeas. When you salt the eggplant and bell pepper before cooking, they cook down well under pressure. Serve the stew over rice, with a generous crumble of feta on top.

1 large eggplant, peeled and cut into ¾-inch pieces

1 red bell pepper, seeded and cut into ¾-inch pieces

1 teaspoon kosher salt

2 tablespoons extra-virgin olive oil

2 garlic cloves, chopped

½ medium yellow onion, diced

1 (15-ounce) can chickpeas, drained and rinsed, or 1½ cups cooked chickpeas (from 4 ounces dried)

2 tablespoons chopped fresh mint

1 teaspoon dried oregano

¼ teaspoon ground cumin

¼ cup water

2 tablespoons tomato paste

½ cup crumbled feta (dairy or plant-based), for serving

3 cups cooked rice, for serving

1. In a mixing bowl, toss the eggplant and bell pepper with the salt. Let sit for 15 minutes.

2. Select the **SAUTÉ** setting on the Instant Pot and heat the olive oil and garlic. When the garlic begins to bubble, add the onion and sauté for about 2 more minutes, until just softened.

3. Add the eggplant and bell pepper, chickpeas, mint, oregano, cumin, and water and stir to combine. Dollop the tomato paste on top, but do not stir.

4. Secure the lid and set the pressure release to **Sealing**. Press the **Cancel** button to reset the cooking program, then select the **PRESSURE COOK** or **MANUAL** setting for 3 minutes at high pressure. (The pot will take about 5 minutes to come up to pressure before the cooking program begins.)

5. When the cooking program ends, perform a quick pressure release by moving the pressure release to **Venting**, or let the pressure release naturally. Open the pot, then stir in the tomato paste.

6. Spoon the stew onto plates or serving bowls. Top with the crumbled feta and serve right away, with rice alongside.

Moroccan-Spiced Vegetable Lentil Stew

A vegan, weeknight-friendly, and simplified take on tagine, the Moroccan catchall term for many different long-simmered stews. This one includes a can of protein-packed lentils, plenty of garlic and ginger, and aromatic cinnamon, coriander, and cumin. A sprinkle of fresh mint, a healthy drizzle of olive oil, and a squeeze of lemon brighten up the flavors.

3 tablespoons extra-virgin olive oil

4 garlic cloves, minced

1-inch piece ginger, peeled and minced

1 red onion, diced

1½ teaspoons ground turmeric

1½ teaspoons ground cinnamon

1½ teaspoons ground coriander

1½ teaspoons kosher salt

½ teaspoon cumin seeds

1¼ cups low-sodium vegetable broth

3 carrots, peeled and cut into bite-size pieces

1 pound gold or red potatoes, cut into bite-size pieces

2 small zucchini (8 ounces), cut into bite-size pieces

1 cup frozen peas

1 cup cherry tomatoes, halved

1. Select the **SAUTÉ** setting on the Instant Pot and heat the olive oil, garlic, and ginger. When the garlic and ginger begin to bubble, add the onion and sauté for about 3 minutes, until it begins to soften. Add the turmeric, cinnamon, coriander, salt, and cumin seeds. Sauté for about 1 more minute, until the spices are aromatic.

2. Stir in the vegetable broth, using a wooden spoon to scrape up any browned bits from the bottom of the pot. Add the carrots, potatoes, zucchini, peas, and tomatoes in even layers. Pour the lentils on top, but do not stir.

3. Secure the lid and set the pressure release to **Sealing**. Press **Cancel** to reset the cooking program, then select the **PRESSURE COOK** or **MANUAL** setting for 3 minutes at high pressure. (The pot will take about 10 minutes to come up to pressure before the cooking program begins.)

4. When the cooking program ends, perform a quick pressure release by moving the pressure valve to **Venting**. Open the pot, add the lemon juice, and gently stir the stew.

1 (15-ounce) can lentils, drained and rinsed *or* 1½ cups cooked lentils (from 4 ounces dried)

1½ tablespoons fresh lemon juice

FOR SERVING

2 tablespoons chopped fresh mint

Extra-virgin olive oil

Lemon wedges

Pita, naan, or other flatbread (gluten-free if preferred)

5. Spoon the stew into serving bowls. Sprinkle on the chopped mint and drizzle generously with olive oil. Serve with lemon wedges and your flatbread of choice on the side.

NOTE: If you have ras el hanout seasoning blend on hand, you can substitute 2 tablespoons of it for the turmeric, cinnamon, and coriander.

Dairy-Free, Gluten-Free (if modified), Vegan   PREP TIME: **5 MINUTES (PLUS 6 HOURS TO SOAK THE PEAS)**   COOK TIME: **20 MINUTES**   YIELD: **6 SERVINGS**

Black-Eyed Pea Succotash Stew

A colorful stew of black-eyed peas and summer vegetables takes less than half an hour to make—just remember to soak the black-eyed peas in a bowl of water in the morning so they'll be ready to cook at dinnertime. You can cook this brightly flavored stew any time of year, using frozen corn and canned tomatoes. Buy a loaf of cornbread or French bread to serve alongside, or bake up a boxed cornbread mix while the stew is cooking.

BLACK-EYED PEAS

8 ounces dried black-eyed peas

4 cups water

1 teaspoon kosher salt

STEW

2 tablespoons extra-virgin olive oil

2 garlic cloves, chopped

1 medium yellow onion, chopped

1 teaspoon kosher salt

½ teaspoon dried thyme

⅛ teaspoon cayenne pepper (optional)

1 cup low-sodium vegetable broth

2 bell peppers, seeded and diced

2 medium zucchini or yellow summer squash (12 ounces), diced

2 cups frozen or fresh corn kernels

1 (14.5-ounce) can petite diced tomatoes and their liquid

1. Soak the black-eyed peas in the water and salt for at least 6 hours, or up to 12 hours. Drain the black-eyed peas and set aside.

2. Select the **SAUTÉ** setting on the Instant Pot and heat the olive oil and garlic. When the garlic is bubbling, add the onion and sauté for 3 minutes, until it is beginning to soften. Add the salt, thyme, and cayenne (if using) and sauté for 1 minute, until aromatic.

3. Add the vegetable broth and black-eyed peas. Stir to combine. Pour in the bell peppers, zucchini, corn, and diced tomatoes in layers, but do not stir.

4. Secure the lid and set the pressure release to **Sealing**. Press **Cancel** to reset the cooking program, then select the **PRESSURE COOK** or **MANUAL** setting for 5 minutes at high pressure. (The pot will take about 10 minutes to come up to pressure before the cooking program begins.)

2 tablespoons chopped fresh flat-leaf parsley

Extra-virgin olive oil

Cornbread or crusty artisan bread (gluten-free if preferred)

5. When the cooking program ends, perform a quick pressure release by moving the pressure release to **Venting**. Open the pot and stir everything together.

6. Spoon the stew into serving bowls. Top each serving with parsley and a generous drizzle of olive oil. Serve right away, with bread alongside.

Dairy-Free, Gluten-Free
(if modified)

PREP TIME: **10 MINUTES**   COOK TIME: **25 MINUTES**   YIELD: **4 SERVINGS**

Shakshuka with Sausage

In this not-so-traditionally-prepared take on shakshuka, the eggs are soft-boiled (well, steamed, really) on a raised metal steam rack rather than poached directly in the sauce, so you end up with lovely, runny yolks while still having the convenience of a pressure-cooked meal. Sausages are simmered in the sauce as well, to make for an extra-hearty dinner. Use whatever link sausages you prefer—merguez is traditional at Dr. Shakshuka, the famed Tel Aviv spot where I first enjoyed this dish, but any smallish links will work well, even breakfast sausage.

1 tablespoon extra-virgin olive oil

12 ounces sausage links

1 yellow onion, thinly sliced

3 garlic cloves, pressed or minced

1 teaspoon ground cumin

1 teaspoon ground coriander

1 (14.5-ounce) can diced tomatoes and their liquid

1 (12-ounce) jar fire-roasted red bell peppers, drained and sliced into strips

½ cup water

4 large eggs

French bread, flatbread, gluten-free bread, or couscous, for serving (see note for couscous preparation)

1. Select the **SAUTÉ** setting on the Instant Pot and heat the olive oil. Add the sausage links and sauté for about 7 minutes, until nicely browned. Transfer the sausages to a dish. Add the onion to the pot and sauté for about 3 minutes, until it begins to soften. Add the garlic, cumin, and coriander and sauté for 1 more minute. Add the tomatoes, bell peppers, and water and stir to combine, using a wooden spoon to nudge any browned bits from the bottom of the pot. Return the sausages to the pot in an even layer on top of the vegetables.

2. Place a 3-inch-tall raised metal steam rack in the pot. Place the eggs on top of the rack.

3. Secure the lid and set the pressure release to **Sealing**. Press the **Cancel** button to reset the cooking program, then select the **PRESSURE COOK** or **MANUAL** setting for 2 minutes at low pressure. (The pot will take about 10 minutes to come up to pressure before the cooking program begins.)

(Continued)

NOTES: If you prefer your eggs hard-boiled, increase the cooking time to 6 minutes.

Use any sausage you like in this recipe. I prefer to use fresh sausages that come in smaller and thinner links, such as merguez or even pork or turkey breakfast sausages. You can also use loose sausage (Italian chicken or turkey sausage or a leaner style of chorizo are good options)— just sauté until cooked through, breaking up the meat as it cooks. If you're using thicker sausages such as andouille or linguica, slice them into ½-inch-thick rounds before cooking.

To make couscous, while the shakshuka cooks, in a heat-proof bowl, stir together 1 cup fine couscous (or 1 [5.8-ounce] box), 1¼ cups boiling water, ½ teaspoon kosher salt (or the spice packet that comes with your boxed couscous), and 1 tablespoon unsalted butter or olive oil. Cover the bowl and let steam while the shakshuka cooks. Fluff with a fork before serving.

4. While the shakshuka is cooking, prepare an ice bath for the eggs.

5. When the cooking program ends, perform a quick pressure release by moving the pressure release to **Venting**. Use a pair of tongs to transfer the eggs to the ice bath and let them cool for about 3 minutes, just until they are cool enough to handle comfortably. Peel the eggs.

6. Remove the steam rack from the pot. Spoon the sausages and tomato-pepper sauce into serving bowls. Top each bowl with one soft-boiled egg. Serve with bread or couscous alongside.

Rosemary-Dijon Chicken and Dumplings

Chicken and dumplings are pure cold weather comfort food, and this version gets a French-inspired flavor boost from fragrant rosemary and tangy Dijon mustard. The addition of a bag of frozen mixed vegetables makes this a nutritious one-pot meal. If you like, you can add a little heavy cream to enrich the thick, flavorful broth.

DUMPLINGS

1½ cups cake flour or all-purpose flour (see note)

1 tablespoon baking powder

¾ teaspoon kosher salt

2 tablespoons unsalted butter (dairy or plant-based), melted

¾ cup milk (dairy or plant-based)

STEW

1 tablespoon extra-virgin olive oil

2 garlic cloves, minced

1 medium yellow onion, diced

3 celery stalks, diced

1½ teaspoons chopped fresh rosemary

½ teaspoon kosher salt

½ teaspoon freshly ground black pepper

1½ pounds boneless, skinless chicken tenders or thighs, cut into 1-inch pieces

1. **Make the dumpling dough:** In a mixing bowl, whisk together the flour, baking powder, and salt. Add the melted butter, then use your fingers to distribute it throughout the flour until it has a crumbly texture.

2. Add the milk. Use a wooden spoon to mix just until the dry ingredients are absorbed. The batter will be thick and lumpy. Set aside.

3. **Make the stew:** Select the **SAUTÉ** setting on the Instant Pot and heat the olive oil and garlic for about 2 minutes, until the garlic is bubbling. Add the onion, celery, rosemary, salt, and pepper and sauté for about 3 minutes, until the onion is beginning to soften.

4. Add the chicken and sauté for about 2 more minutes, until the chicken pieces are mostly opaque on the outside (they do not have to be cooked through). Stir in the Dijon mustard and chicken broth, using a wooden spoon to nudge any browned bits off the bottom of the pot.

(Continued)

2 tablespoons Dijon mustard

2 cups low-sodium chicken broth

1 (12-ounce) bag frozen mixed vegetables, thawed

¼ cup chopped fresh flat-leaf parsley

¼ cup heavy cream (optional)

NOTE: Cake flour yields more tender dumplings, while all-purpose flour results in chewier, denser dumplings.

5. Use a 1½-tablespoon cookie scoop to portion out the dumplings, dropping them into the pot on top of the vegetables and broth in a single layer.

6. Secure the lid and set the pressure release to **Sealing**. Press **Cancel** to reset the cooking program, then select the **PRESSURE COOK** or **MANUAL** setting for 8 minutes at high pressure. (The pot will take about 5 minutes to come up to pressure before the cooking program begins.)

7. When the cooking program ends, let the pressure release naturally for 10 minutes, then move the pressure release to **Venting** to release any remaining steam.

8. Open the pot. Add the thawed mixed vegetables, parsley, and cream (if using) and stir gently to combine, taking care not to break up the dumplings.

9. Ladle into bowls and serve right away.

Dairy-Free, Gluten-Free
(if modified)

PREP TIME: **5 MINUTES**   COOK TIME: **35 MINUTES**   YIELD: **6 SERVINGS**

Smoky Chicken and White Bean Stew with Gremolata

Smoked paprika lends its earthy flavor to this filling chicken and bean stew, and lemon juice and a gremolata of parsley, lemon zest, and chopped garlic perk it up at the end of cooking. Serve it with some crusty bread or flatbread alongside—you'll want something to sop up the flavorful, thick broth.

1 tablespoon extra-virgin olive oil

1 medium yellow onion, diced

3 carrots, cut into ½-inch-thick rounds

2 celery stalks, diced

1½ pounds boneless, skinless chicken thighs, cut into bite-size pieces

1½ teaspoons kosher salt

1½ teaspoons smoked paprika

1 teaspoon poultry seasoning

½ teaspoon freshly ground black pepper

½ cup low-sodium chicken broth

1 (15-ounce) can white beans, drained and rinsed, *or* 1½ cups cooked beans (from 4 ounces dried)

2 tablespoons tomato paste

1. Select the **SAUTÉ** setting on the Instant Pot and heat the olive oil. Add the onion, carrots, and celery and sauté for about 5 minutes, until the onion is softened and translucent.

2. Add the chicken and sauté for 3 more minutes, until the chicken is mostly opaque on the outside. It does not have to be cooked through.

3. Add the salt, paprika, poultry seasoning, pepper, and chicken broth and use a wooden spoon to nudge any browned bits from the bottom of the pot. Pour in the white beans, then dollop the tomato paste on top, but do not stir.

4. Secure the lid and set the pressure release to **Sealing**. Press the **Cancel** button to reset the cooking program, then select the **PRESSURE COOK** or **MANUAL** setting for 10 minutes at high pressure. (The pot will take about 5 minutes to come up to pressure before the cooking program begins.)

(Continued)

GREMOLATA

¼ cup fresh flat-leaf parsley leaves

Grated zest of ½ lemon

2 garlic cloves, peeled

2 tablespoons fresh lemon juice

FOR SERVING

Extra-virgin olive oil

Freshly ground black pepper

Crusty artisan bread or flatbread (gluten-free if preferred)

5. **While the stew is cooking, make the gremolata:** Place the parsley in a pile on a cutting board and top with the lemon zest and garlic cloves. Chop until everything is finely chopped and combined.

6. When the cooking program ends, let the pressure release naturally for at least 10 minutes, then move the pressure release to **Venting** to release any remaining steam. Open the pot and stir in the lemon juice and gremolata.

7. Ladle the stew into serving bowls. Drizzle generously with olive oil, top with a few grinds of pepper, and serve right away, with bread or flatbread for dunking.

Ground Turkey Chili Verde with Corn and Zucchini

Every once in a while, I prefer to make my chili without beans, and this ground turkey version is a nice change from the usual bean-free beef versions you'll find. I use a jar of salsa verde and a bag of frozen corn to keep things weeknight-friendly and save some time. Served with some warmed tortillas alongside, it's a high-protein, veggie-packed meal that my whole family enjoys. If you like, you can add more toppings to your bowl, such as sliced avocado, chopped onion, fresh cilantro, and/or sour cream.

1 tablespoon extra-virgin olive oil

3 garlic cloves, chopped

1½ pounds ground turkey (93% lean or turkey breast) or plant-based chicken grinds (see note)

1 large yellow onion, diced

2 poblano chiles, seeded and diced

1 green bell pepper

2 teaspoons dried oregano

2 teaspoons ground coriander

1 teaspoon ground cumin

1 teaspoon kosher salt

1 medium zucchini, diced

1 (1-pound) bag frozen corn kernels, thawed

1 (16-ounce) jar salsa verde (tomatillo-based)

¼ cup chopped fresh cilantro

1. Select the **SAUTÉ** setting on the Instant Pot and heat the olive oil and garlic. When the garlic is bubbling, add the ground turkey and sauté until the meat is cooked through and no pink traces remain, about 6 minutes, breaking it up with a spoon as it cooks.

2. Stir in the onion, diced chiles, bell pepper, oregano, coriander, cumin, and salt. Sauté for another 3 minutes, until the onion is beginning to soften. Stir in the zucchini, corn, and salsa verde.

3. Secure the lid and set the pressure release to **Sealing**. Press the **Cancel** button to reset the cooking program, then select the **PRESSURE COOK** or **MANUAL** setting for 15 minutes at high pressure. (It will take about 10 minutes for the pot to come up to pressure before the cooking program begins.)

(Continued)

1 cup shredded Monterey Jack cheese or Mexican cheese blend (dairy or plant-based)

8 corn tortillas or tostadas, warmed

4. When the cooking program ends, let the pressure release naturally for at least 10 minutes, then move the pressure release to **Venting** to release any remaining steam.

5. Open the pot and stir in the chopped cilantro. Taste for seasoning, adding salt if needed.

6. Ladle the chili into bowls and serve it hot, topped with grated cheese, with warm tortillas alongside.

NOTES: My preferred meatless substitute to use here is the Emerge Plant-Based Chik'n Grinds from Kroger's Simple Truth line. They're sold in the meat department, near the Beyond Meat, Impossible, and other refrigerated plant-based meat substitutes. They are vegan but not gluten-free. Alternatively, substitute 3 cups cooked white beans or pinto beans for the chick'n, adding them with the zucchini, corn, and salsa verde.

Japanese-Style Ground Beef and Potato Stew

Nikujaga, which literally translates from Japanese to "meat and potatoes," is a dish that's traditionally simmered on the stove until most of the broth has boiled away, then served with rice and miso soup alongside. When made in the Instant Pot, the stew turns out more brothy, so I forgo the miso soup and serve it simply with rice. Shirataki noodles are a naturally low-carb addition, but you can use ramen if you prefer (see the recipe note below).

1 pound ground beef (90% or leaner) or plant-based beef grinds

1 yellow onion, cut into ½-inch wedges

3 carrots, peeled and roll-cut into 1-inch pieces

1½ pounds Yukon Gold potatoes, peeled and cut into 1½-inch pieces

2 cups dashi (see note) or low-sodium vegetable broth

¼ cup mirin

¼ cup soy sauce or tamari

1 package spaghetti-style tofu shirataki noodles, rinsed and blanched according to package instructions

1 cup frozen peas

Cooked rice, for serving

1. Select the **SAUTÉ** setting on the Instant Pot and add the ground beef. Sauté for about 5 minutes, breaking up the meat with a wooden spoon or spatula as it cooks, until no pink streaks remain.

2. Add the onion and sauté for 2 more minutes, until it starts to soften.

3. Add the carrots, potatoes, dashi, mirin, soy sauce, and noodles. Stir to combine, using a wooden spoon to scrape any browned bits from the bottom of the pot.

4. Secure the lid and set the pressure release to **Sealing**. Press the **Cancel** button to reset the cooking program, then select the **PRESSURE COOK** or **MANUAL** setting for 5 minutes at high pressure. (The pot will take about 10 minutes to come up to pressure before the cooking program begins.)

NOTES: Shirataki noodles can be found refrigerated, near the tofu, in most larger supermarkets. I like the ones from House Foods brand. I prefer the texture of the ones with tofu added, but the plain variety is more traditional in this dish.

If you'd like to use ramen noodles instead of shirataki, cook them separately, then stir them in with the peas, after pressure cooking.

Dashi powder can be found at most Asian grocery stores and online. I like the Kuze Fuku & Sons brand, which I get at Costco. It comes in tea bag–like sachets that you simmer in boiling water for a couple minutes.

5. When the cooking program ends, perform a quick pressure release by moving the pressure release to **Venting**. Add the peas and stir to combine.

6. Ladle the stew into serving bowls and serve with bowls of rice on the side.

Tempeh or Beef Chili

Whether you use tempeh or ground beef, this chili hits all the flavor notes of a classic chili con carne, cooked at weeknight speed in under an hour. In my house, we like to serve ours topped with Fritos, diced onion, and shredded cheese, and sometimes we add a dollop of sour cream or some sliced avocado for extra richness. You can stretch this meal by serving it over some rice if you like, too.

2 tablespoons extra-virgin olive oil

1 yellow onion, chopped

1 green bell pepper, chopped

2 garlic cloves, chopped

2 (8-ounce) packages tempeh (gluten-free if preferred), broken into 1-inch pieces, *or* 1 pound ground beef (90% or leaner) or plant-based beef grinds

3 tablespoons chili powder

1½ teaspoons kosher salt

1 teaspoon dried oregano

1 teaspoon ground coriander

1 teaspoon ground cumin

1 (15-ounce) can pinto or kidney beans, drained and rinsed, *or* 1½ cups cooked beans (from 4 ounces dried)

1 cup low-sodium vegetable or beef broth

1 (14.5-ounce) can petite diced tomatoes and their liquid

2 tablespoons tomato paste

1. Select the **SAUTÉ** setting and heat the olive oil in the Instant Pot. Add the onion, bell pepper, and garlic and sauté for 5 minutes, until the onion is softened and translucent.

2. Add the tempeh or ground beef and sauté for 5 minutes (or until no longer pink if using beef), using a spoon or spatula to break up the tempeh or meat as it cooks. Stir in the chili powder, salt, oregano, coriander, and cumin and sauté for 1 more minute.

3. Add the beans and broth. Stir to combine. Pour in the diced tomatoes, then dollop the tomato paste on top, but do not stir.

4. Secure the lid and set the pressure release to **Sealing**. Press the **Cancel** button to reset the cooking program, then select the **PRESSURE COOK** or **MANUAL** setting for 10 minutes at high pressure. (The pot will take about 5 minutes to come up to pressure before the cooking program begins.)

5. When the cooking program ends, let the pressure release naturally for 10 minutes, then move the pressure release to **Venting** to release any remaining steam.

(Continued)

1½ cups shredded Mexican cheese blend (dairy or plant-based)

¾ cup diced red or white onion

1 (6-ounce) bag Fritos or tortilla chips

6. Open the pot. To thicken the chili, leave the pot uncovered, select the **SAUTÉ** setting, and let the chili simmer and reduce for 10 minutes. (Don't stir the chili while it's reducing, or it will tend to splatter.)

7. Wearing heat-proof mitts, remove the inner pot from the Instant Pot housing. Let the chili sit in the pot for 5 more minutes, then stir, using a wooden spoon to nudge any browned bits from the bottom of the pot.

8. Ladle the chili into serving bowls. Top with shredded cheese, diced onion, and Fritos and serve right away.

NOTES: You can cook white rice (long-grain or basmati works well) on top of the chili, pot-in-pot style, if you like, to serve with the chili. Follow the directions for this method in the recipe note on page 62.

To make chili dogs, heat hot dogs in the air fryer for 5 minutes at 400°F. If you'd like your buns toasted, add them to the air frying basket when the **Turn food** notice comes on. Serve the hot dogs in buns, with about ¼ cup chili ladled on top of each hot dog. Sprinkle 2 tablespoons shredded cheddar cheese and a tablespoon or two diced yellow or white onion on each hot dog, and serve right away.

Cod and Potato Stew

Fish stew isn't always my first thought for dinner, but when I make it, I'm so glad that I did. It can't be beat for ease and last-minute convenience, since you can use fish fillets straight from the freezer. This recipe is inspired by Basque fish and potato stews, which are often on the brothy side. In the final few minutes of the pressure release, use your air fryer to toast up some crusty bread to serve alongside and soak up the delicious broth.

3 tablespoons extra-virgin olive oil

2 garlic cloves, minced or pressed

1 yellow onion, diced

1 red bell pepper, seeded and diced

1 jalapeño chile, seeded and minced (optional)

½ teaspoon kosher salt

¼ teaspoon red pepper flakes (optional)

1¼ pounds Yukon Gold potatoes, diced

1 (14-ounce) can petite diced tomatoes and their liquid

2 cups low-sodium chicken broth

1 pound fresh or frozen cod fillets

2 tablespoons chopped fresh flat-leaf parsley

Crusty artisan bread or gluten-free bread, toasted, for serving

1. Select the **SAUTÉ** setting on the Instant Pot and add the olive oil and garlic. When the garlic is bubbling and golden (after about 2 minutes), add the onion, bell pepper, jalapeño, salt, and pepper flakes. Sauté for 5 more minutes, until the onion is softened.

2. Add the potatoes, tomatoes, and broth and stir to combine. Add the cod fillets on top in as even a layer as possible (it's fine if they overlap a bit).

3. Secure the lid and set the pressure release to **Sealing**. Press the **Cancel** button to reset the cooking program, then select the **PRESSURE COOK** or **MANUAL** setting for 2 minutes at high pressure if using fresh fish or 5 minutes at high pressure if using frozen fish. (The pot will take about 15 minutes to come up to pressure before the cooking program begins.)

(Continued)

4. When the cooking program ends, let the pressure release naturally for 15 minutes, then move the pressure release to **Venting** to release any remaining steam.

5. Open the pot. Stir the parsley into the stew, using a spoon to break up the cod into bite-size chunks.

6. Ladle the stew into serving bowls and serve with bread on the side.

CHAPTER 5

ONE & DONE DINNERS

Dairy-Free, Gluten-Free, Vegan (if modified)   PREP TIME: **5 MINUTES**   COOK TIME: **35 MINUTES**   YIELD: **3 TO 4 SERVINGS**

Red Beans and Rice

This simple Cajun-inspired pot of rice, beans, and sausage makes for a filling weeknight staple. It's savory and full of protein from beans and sausages—you can add spicy andouille, milder kielbasa, or the plant-based links of your choice for a vegan meal. A topping of green onions and plenty of hot sauce are all you need to enjoy a bowl.

1 tablespoon extra-virgin olive oil

1 garlic clove, minced

1 small yellow onion, diced

2 celery stalks, diced

1 green bell pepper, seeded and diced

8 ounces fully cooked smoked and/or spicy sausage (such as andouille or kielbasa) or plant-based sausage links, sliced or diced

1 cup long-grain white rice or quick-cooking brown rice

1 (15-ounce) can kidney beans, drained and rinsed, *or* 1½ cups cooked beans (from 4 ounces dried)

¾ teaspoon Old Bay seasoning

1 cup low-sodium vegetable or chicken broth

¼ cup water

1 green onion, thinly sliced, for serving

Hot sauce (such as Frank's RedHot or Crystal), for serving

1. Select the **SAUTÉ** setting on the Instant Pot and heat the olive oil and garlic for about 1 minute, until the garlic is bubbling. Add the onion, celery, and bell pepper and cook for 3 more minutes. Add the sausage and sauté for another 3 minutes or so, until it is warmed through and a bit browned.

2. Add the rice, beans, Old Bay, broth, and water and stir to combine, using a wooden spoon to nudge any browned bits from the bottom of the pot.

3. Secure the lid and set the pressure release to **Sealing**. Press the **Cancel** button to reset the cooking program, then select the **PRESSURE COOK** or **MANUAL** setting for 10 minutes at high pressure. (The pot will take about 5 minutes to come up to pressure before the cooking program begins.)

4. When the cooking program ends, let the pressure release naturally for 10 minutes, then move the pressure release to **Venting** to release any remaining steam. Open the pot and stir.

5. Spoon the rice and beans into serving bowls. Sprinkle with green onions and serve with hot sauce.

NOTE: If you'd like to make a bigger pot of rice and beans, this recipe is easily doubled. The cooking time will remain the same.

Brazilian-Style Black Bean Stew and Rice

This recipe owes its inspiration to Brazilian feijoada, but it's far from traditional. For one thing, it's made with poultry products rather than red meat—turkey kielbasa, chicken breast, and turkey bacon take the place of beef and pork for a lightened-up, brothy take on this classic Brazilian dish. The rice cooks separately in a bowl on top of the stew (both in the Instant Pot), so you'll have everything ready to go at once. Serve orange wedges alongside for a refreshing counterpoint to the hearty stew.

1½ cups water

1½ cups long-grain white rice

½ teaspoon kosher salt

1 tablespoon extra-virgin olive oil

4 slices turkey bacon, diced

1 yellow onion, diced

2 garlic cloves, minced

1 pound boneless, skinless chicken breasts, cut into bite-size pieces

2 cups chicken broth

1 (13-ounce) package turkey kielbasa, cut into ½-inch-thick rounds

2 (15-ounce) cans black beans, drained and rinsed, *or* 1½ cups cooked beans (from 4 ounces dried)

1 bay leaf

1. Add the water, rice, and salt to a 1½-quart stainless-steel bowl.

2. Select the **SAUTÉ** setting on the Instant Pot and heat the olive oil. Add the bacon and sauté for 2 minutes, until it is beginning to brown. Add the onion and garlic and sauté for 3 more minutes, until the onion begins to soften. Add the chicken and sauté for 3 more minutes, until it is opaque on the outside (it does not have to be cooked all the way through).

3. Add the broth and use a wooden spoon to scrape any browned bits from the bottom of the pot. Add the kielbasa, black beans, and bay leaf and stir to combine.

4. Add a raised metal steam rack to the pot, then place the rice bowl on the rack.

5. Secure the lid and set the pressure release to **Sealing**. Select the **PRESSURE COOK** or **MANUAL** setting for 10 minutes

(Continued)

2 tablespoons chopped fresh flat-leaf parsley or cilantro, for serving

3 oranges, cut into wedges, for serving

Hot sauce, for serving

at high pressure. (The pot will take about 10 minutes to come up to pressure before the cooking program begins.)

6. When the cooking program ends, let the pressure naturally release for at least 10 minutes, then move the pressure release to **Venting** to release any remaining steam.

7. Open the pot. Wearing heat-resistant mitts, remove the rice bowl and steam rack. Remove and discard the bay leaf.

8. Use a fork to fluff the rice. Ladle the stew into serving bowls and top with the parsley. Serve with the rice and orange wedges on the side, with hot sauce at the table.

Coconut Butter Chicken or Chickpeas and Cumin Rice

Butter chicken is one of the most popular Indian takeout recipes for a reason—it is delicious and adored by children and adults alike (I can attest that my toddler is a huge fan). In this dairy-free version, a generous amount of spice is tempered by rich coconut milk and coconut oil, making a tomato-based "cream" sauce for the tender pieces of chicken breast. A bowl of cumin seed–speckled basmati rice cooks right on top of the chicken, so dinner is ready all at once. Look to the recipe note on page 124 for a vegan version made with chickpeas.

RICE

1 cup water

1 cup white or quick-cooking basmati rice

½ teaspoon cumin seeds

¼ teaspoon kosher salt

CHICKEN

¼ cup water

1 (14.5-ounce) can no-salt-added petite diced tomatoes and their liquid

4 garlic cloves, peeled

1-inch piece ginger, peeled and minced

1½ teaspoons garam masala, divided

1½ teaspoons kosher salt

1 teaspoon ground cumin

1 teaspoon smoked paprika

1. **Prepare the rice:** In a 1½-quart stainless-steel bowl, combine the water, rice, cumin seeds, and salt. Set aside.

2. **Make the chicken:** Add the water, tomatoes, garlic, ginger, 1 teaspoon of the garam masala, salt, cumin, paprika, turmeric, and cayenne to the Instant Pot and stir to combine. Add the chicken on top of the tomato mixture in a single layer.

3. Place a raised metal steam rack in the pot, then place the bowl of rice on the rack.

4. Secure the lid and set the pressure release to **Sealing**. Select the **PRESSURE COOK** or **MANUAL** setting for 10 minutes at high pressure. (The pot will take about 10 minutes to come up to pressure before the cooking program begins.)

5. When the cooking program ends, let the pressure release naturally for 10 minutes, then move the pressure release to **Venting** to release any remaining steam.

(Continued)

1 teaspoon ground turmeric

½ teaspoon cayenne pepper

1½ pounds boneless, skinless chicken breasts, cut into 2-inch pieces

½ cup roughly chopped fresh cilantro, plus 1 tablespoon for garnish

½ cup coconut milk

¼ cup coconut oil

NOTES: To up the vegetable quotient in this recipe, you can stir in a 5-ounce bag of baby spinach or baby kale when you add the shredded chicken and blended sauce back to the pot. Warm on the **SAUTÉ** setting, stirring often, until the spinach has wilted and everything is heated through.

To make a vegan version of this dish, replace the chicken with 2 (15-ounce) cans chickpeas, drained and rinsed (or 3 cups cooked chickpeas, from 8 ounces dried). When the cooking program ends, perform the 10-minute natural pressure release as written, remove the bowl of rice and the steam rack, and add the cilantro, coconut milk, coconut oil, and remaining garam masala to the chickpeas. Stir to combine. Fluff the rice and serve it with the chickpeas. Note that with this variation, the sauce will remain a bit chunkier in texture, since you'll be omitting the blending step.

6. Open the pot and, wearing heat-resistant mitts, remove the bowl of rice and the steam rack. Using tongs, transfer the chicken pieces to a dish.

7. Press the **Cancel** button to reset the cooking program, then select the **SAUTÉ** setting. Let the sauce simmer uncovered for about 10 minutes, stirring occasionally, until the mixture has thickened a bit and reduced to approximately 2¼ cups.

8. While the sauce is reducing, use two forks to shred the chicken into bite-size pieces.

9. When the sauce has reduced, turn off the pot. Transfer the sauce to a blender, along with the cilantro, coconut milk, coconut oil, and remaining ½ teaspoon garam masala. Blend at high speed for 30 seconds, until smooth. (Alternatively, you can blend the sauce in the Instant Pot inner pot using an immersion blender. Be sure to fully submerge the blender head to prevent splattering.)

10. Return the sauce and chicken to the Instant Pot and stir to combine. Use the **SAUTÉ** setting to warm everything through until bubbling, about 2 minutes. Turn off the pot.

11. Fluff the rice with a fork. Spoon the chicken and sauce onto serving plates, garnish with the cilantro, and serve right away, with the rice on the side.

Picadillo and Rice

Picadillo is a popular dish in many Latin American countries, and this version is a speedy take on the Cuban-style version. A mixture of ground beef and vegetables is simmered in a tomato-based sauce that includes olives and raisins for a salty/sweet contrast. When we have these sorts of one-pot meals in my house, I'll either cook rice in a bowl in the Instant Pot on top of the main dish (see the recipe note below) or heat up a package of frozen cauliflower rice in the microwave, for a lower-carb option.

1 pound ground beef (90% or leaner) or plant-based beef grinds

½ teaspoon kosher salt

¼ teaspoon ground black pepper

1 medium red onion, diced

1 large red bell pepper, diced

2 Roma or plum tomatoes, diced

2 garlic cloves, diced

¼ cup chopped fresh cilantro, plus 2 tablespoons for serving

½ cup water

¼ cup green olives, plus 2 tablespoons brine

¾ teaspoon ground cumin

2 bay leaves

¼ cup raisins (optional)

3 tablespoons tomato paste

3 cups cooked rice or cauliflower rice

1 large avocado, for serving

1. Select the **SAUTÉ** setting on the Instant Pot and let it preheat for 2 minutes. Add the ground beef, salt, and pepper and sauté, breaking up the meat with a spoon as it cooks, for about 5 minutes, until no longer pink.

2. Add the onion, bell peppers, tomatoes, garlic, and cilantro. Sauté for about 3 minutes, until the onion begins to soften. Add the water, olives and brine, cumin, and bay leaves and stir to combine, using a wooden spoon to nudge loose any browned bits from the bottom of the pot. Sprinkle the raisins (if using) over the meat and vegetables, then dollop the tomato paste on top, but do not stir.

3. Secure the lid and set the pressure release to **Sealing**. Press the **Cancel** button to reset the cooking program, then select the **PRESSURE COOK** or **MANUAL** setting for 10 minutes at high pressure. (The pot will take about 5 minutes to come up to pressure before the cooking program begins.)

(Continued)

4. When the cooking program ends, perform a quick pressure release by moving the pressure release to **Venting**, or let the pressure release naturally.

5. Open the pot, then select the **SAUTÉ** setting. Let the picadillo simmer uncovered for 6 to 8 minutes, stirring occasionally, until the mixture has thickened enough that you can see the bottom of the pot momentarily when stirring.

6. Turn off the pot. Spoon the picadillo onto serving plates, sprinkle the cilantro on top, and serve right away, with rice or cauliflower rice and sliced avocado alongside.

NOTES: If you like, you can cook long-grain white rice or quick-cooking brown rice at the same time as the picadillo. Before you turn on the Instant Pot, in a 1½-quart stainless-steel bowl, stir together 1 cup rice and 1 cup water and set aside. After adding the raisins and tomato paste to the picadillo, place a raised metal steam rack in the pot, then place the bowl of rice on top.

For a variation on sloppy joes, serve the picadillo on kaiser rolls or hamburger buns, with avocado slices on top.

Dairy-Free (if modified),
Gluten-Free (if modified),
Vegan (if modified)

PREP TIME: **5 MINUTES**   COOK TIME: **20 MINUTES**   YIELD: **4 SERVINGS**

Helpful Hamburger with Chickpea Macaroni and Cheddar

Hearty comfort food in a flash is the name of the game with this cheesy, savory, high-protein dish of pasta and ground beef. It cooks up in just 20 minutes and uses gluten-free chickpea-based pasta. For a vegan version, you'll use a ground beef substitute and plant-based shredded cheddar. Serve it up on its own or with a green salad alongside.

1 tablespoon extra virgin olive oil

2 garlic cloves, minced or pressed

½ medium yellow onion, diced

1 pound ground beef (90% or leaner) or plant-based beef grinds

2 cups low-sodium vegetable or beef broth

8 ounces chickpea macaroni (such as Banza)

1 teaspoon Worcestershire sauce (gluten-free if preferred)

½ teaspoon kosher salt

½ teaspoon freshly ground black pepper

2 tablespoons tomato paste

1 cup shredded cheddar cheese (dairy or plant-based)

1 cup frozen peas, thawed (optional)

1 tablespoon chopped fresh flat-leaf parsley, for serving (optional)

1. Select the **SAUTÉ** setting on the Instant Pot and add the olive oil and garlic. When the garlic begins to bubble, add the onion and sauté for 2 minutes, until the onion begins to soften. Add the beef and sauté for about 5 more minutes, breaking up the meat with a wooden spoon, until no traces of pink remain.

2. Add the broth, then use a wooden spoon to scrape any browned bits from the bottom of the pot. Stir in the macaroni, Worcestershire, salt, and pepper. Dollop the tomato paste on top, but do not stir.

3. Secure the lid and set the pressure release to **Sealing**. Press the **Cancel** button, then select the **PRESSURE COOK** or **MANUAL** setting for 4 minutes at high pressure. (The pot will take about 5 minutes to come up to pressure before the cooking program begins.)

4. When the cooking program ends, perform a quick pressure release by moving the pressure release to **Venting**. Open the

(Continued)

NOTE: You can also make this recipe with regular or whole-wheat macaroni. If using whole-wheat macaroni, increase the cooking time to 5 minutes.

pot, add the cheese and peas (if using), and gently stir until the cheese is melted and everything is evenly combined.

5. Ladle the macaroni into bowls, sprinkle with the parsley (if using), and serve right away.

Dairy-Free, Gluten-Free (if modified), Vegan (if modified)   PREP TIME: **5 MINUTES**   COOK TIME: **15 MINUTES**   YIELD: **3 TO 4 SERVINGS**

Chicken or Soy Curl Fajitas

An air fryer makes quick work of fajita night, and best of all, you've only got to give the chicken and peppers one stir during cooking, rather than standing over the stove. They're similar to a sheet pan dinner, except that the air fryer preheats and cooks much faster than a traditional oven. We enjoy these with simple accompaniments of lime wedges and hot sauce, but you're welcome to jazz them up with other fixings such as shredded cheese, sour cream, and sliced avocado. Look to the recipe note below for a vegan variation using soy curls.

1 pound boneless, skinless chicken thighs or breasts, cut into ½-inch strips

1 red bell pepper, seeded and sliced into strips

1 green bell pepper, seeded and sliced into strips

1 yellow onion, sliced

1 tablespoon chili powder

1 teaspoon kosher salt

½ teaspoon ground cumin

½ teaspoon garlic powder

2 tablespoons extra-virgin olive oil

FOR SERVING

Fajita-size tortillas (gluten-free if preferred), warmed

Lime wedges

Hot sauce (Cholula or Tapatío)

1. Preheat the air fryer on **BAKE** at 400°F and set the cooking time for 15 minutes. If using a toaster oven–style air fryer, line the cooking pan with parchment paper or aluminum foil.

2. Add the chicken, bell peppers, and onion to a mixing bowl. Sprinkle them with the chili powder, salt, cumin, and garlic powder, then drizzle in the olive oil. Toss to coat evenly.

3. Spread out the chicken and vegetables on the lined cooking pan, or if using a basket-style air fryer, in the air frying basket.

4. Bake the fajitas in the preheated air fryer. When the **Turn food** notice comes on (or two-thirds of the way through the cooking time), give everything a stir.

5. Serve the fajitas in the tortillas, with lime wedges and hot sauce on the side.

NOTE: You can substitute Butler's Soy Curls for the chicken in this recipe. Use 4 ounces soy curls (½ bag), hydrated according to the package instructions. Reduce the cooking time to 10 minutes.

Herb-Roasted Chicken, Potatoes, and Brussels Sprouts

A simple, pantry-based blend of herbs, spices, and olive oil is all you need to flavor juicy chicken thighs and tender, well-browned potatoes, and Brussels sprouts. Serve this air fryer dinner anytime you need a meal in a flash.

4 boneless, skinless chicken thighs

1 pound creamer/baby/petite potatoes (halved if larger than 1 inch in diameter)

12 ounces Brussels sprouts, halved if large

1½ teaspoons seasoned salt

1 teaspoon Italian seasoning or poultry seasoning

1 teaspoon garlic powder

1 teaspoon paprika

½ teaspoon freshly ground black pepper

2 tablespoons extra-virgin olive oil

NOTE: If you like, you can replace the potatoes and Brussels sprouts with up to 1¾ pounds of any other hardy vegetables you like, cut into 1-inch pieces. Carrots, parsnips, sweet potatoes, turnips, and winter squash are good options.

1. Preheat the air fryer on **ROAST** to 400°F and set the cooking time for 20 minutes. If using a toaster oven–style air fryer, line the cooking pan with parchment paper or aluminum foil.

2. Add the chicken thighs, potatoes, and Brussels sprouts to a large mixing bowl. Sprinkle in the seasoned salt, Italian seasoning, garlic powder, paprika, and pepper, then drizzle in the olive oil. Use your hands to toss and mix until the chicken and vegetables are evenly coated with the spices and oil.

3. Spread out the chicken and vegetables in a single layer on the lined cooking pan or, if using a basket-style air fryer, in the air frying basket.

4. Roast the chicken and vegetables in the preheated air fryer.

5. When the cooking program ends, transfer the chicken and vegetables to plates and serve right away.

NOTE: If your chicken thighs are on the larger side (6 ounces each), increase the cooking time to 23 minutes. Use an instant-read thermometer to make sure they're cooked to at least 165°F at their thickest part.

Jerk-Spiced Salmon, Tomatoes, and Sweet Potatoes

Make your own homemade jerk seasoning blend, then use a couple tablespoons to spice up a dinner of salmon, tomatoes, and sweet potatoes. This recipe makes enough seasoning blend for five meals, and it's also good on chicken, tofu, and other kinds of fish.

JERK SEASONING

2 tablespoons brown sugar

1 tablespoon kosher salt

1 tablespoon poultry seasoning

1 tablespoon dried thyme

1 tablespoon freshly ground black pepper

1 tablespoon ground allspice

1 tablespoon onion powder

2 teaspoons garlic powder

1 teaspoon ground cinnamon

1 teaspoon ground nutmeg

1 teaspoon ground ginger

1 teaspoon cayenne pepper

SALMON AND VEGETABLES

1 (1-pound) salmon fillet (skinless or skin-on)

1 pint cherry or grape tomatoes

1 (1-pound) sweet potato, peeled and cut into ¾-inch pieces

2 tablespoons extra-virgin olive oil

1. **Make the jerk seasoning:** In a bowl, mix together the brown sugar, salt, herbs, and spices. Transfer to a tightly lidded jar. The seasoning will keep in a tightly lidded container in the pantry for up to 1 year.

2. **Make the salmon and vegetables:** Preheat the air fryer on **BAKE** at 375°F and set the cooking time for 18 minutes. If using a toaster oven–style air fryer, line the cooking pan with parchment paper.

3. Place the salmon fillet in the middle of the cooking pan or, if using a basket-style air fryer, in the air frying basket. Arrange the tomatoes and sweet potatoes around the salmon in a single layer.

4. Sprinkle 2 tablespoons of the jerk seasoning blend evenly over the salmon and vegetables, then drizzle on the olive oil.

5. Bake the salmon, tomatoes, and sweet potatoes in the preheated air fryer.

6. When the cooking program ends, use a spatula to portion the salmon into quarters. Transfer the salmon to serving plates, along with the tomatoes and sweet potatoes. Serve right away.

Dairy-Free (if modified),
Vegan (if modified)
PREP TIME: **5 MINUTES**
COOK TIME: **30 MINUTES**
YIELD: **4 TO 6 SERVINGS**

Whole-Wheat Spaghetti in Meaty Ragù

Use ground turkey, chicken, beef, or plant-based meat grinds in this recipe for the easiest spaghetti with meat sauce you've ever made. Store-bought marinara gets the job done—just use whichever one you like best. I like to use whole-wheat spaghetti since it holds up well and still has a nice chew even after pressure cooking. Shorter pastas like penne and macaroni work nicely, too.

1 tablespoon extra-virgin olive oil

2 garlic cloves, minced

1 medium yellow onion, diced

½ teaspoon kosher salt

1 teaspoon Italian seasoning

½ teaspoon red pepper flakes (optional)

1 pound ground turkey, chicken, beef (90% or leaner), or plant-based meat grinds

1 pound whole-wheat spaghetti

4 cups water

1 (25-ounce) jar marinara sauce

2 tablespoons tomato paste

Fresh basil leaves, for serving

Shredded or grated parmesan (dairy or plant-based), for serving

1. Select the **SAUTÉ** setting on the Instant Pot and heat the olive oil and garlic for about 1 minute, until the garlic is bubbling. Add the onion and salt and sauté for about 3 more minutes, until the onions are beginning to soften. Add the Italian seasoning and red pepper flakes (if using) and sauté for another 30 seconds or so, until aromatic.

2. Add the ground meat. Sauté for about 5 minutes, breaking up the meat with a spatula as it cooks, until no traces of pink remain.

3. Break the spaghetti noodles in half and add them to the pot, spreading them out on top of the ground meat mixture in an even layer.

4. Pour the water over the spaghetti, then pour the spaghetti sauce on top. Use a wooden spoon to poke down any noodles that aren't submerged in the liquid, until all are fully covered. Add the tomato paste in a dollop on top, but do not stir.

5. Secure the lid and set the pressure release to **Sealing**. Press **Cancel** to reset the cooking program, then select the

PRESSURE COOK or **MANUAL** setting for 5 minutes at high pressure. (The pot will take about 10 minutes to come up to pressure before the cooking program begins.)

6. When the cooking program ends, perform a quick pressure release by moving the pressure release to **Venting**.

7. Open the pot. Stir the noodles into the sauce, using a spoon or spatula to break up any clumps of noodles. It might look like there is too much liquid initially, but it will absorb. Let the pasta sit for 5 minutes, stir it once more, then spoon it into serving bowls and serve with basil and parmesan on top.

NOTES: To help prevent the spaghetti from clumping together too much, I like to spread them out, a quarter of the noodles at a time, in opposite directions as I'm adding them to the pot.

For spicier spaghetti, substitute arrabbiata or puttanesca sauce for the marinara.

Dairy-Free (if modified), Vegan (if modified)   PREP TIME: **10 MINUTES**   COOK TIME: **40 MINUTES**   YIELD: **6 SERVINGS**

Beef and Bulgur–Stuffed Peppers

This recipe makes use of the Instant Pot to make the beef and bulgur wheat filling and the air fryer to cook the stuffed peppers and brown their cheesy topping. Buy the largest bell peppers you can find—the filling makes a generous amount, so you'll want plenty of room to stuff it into your peppers! Extra filling can be served on its own in a bowl as leftovers, too.

1 tablespoon extra-virgin olive oil

2 garlic cloves, chopped

1 medium yellow onion, diced

1 pound ground beef (90% or leaner) or plant-based beef grinds

1 teaspoon Italian seasoning

1 teaspoon kosher salt

¼ teaspoon freshly ground black pepper

1 cup low-sodium beef or vegetable broth

1 cup bulgur wheat

1 (8-ounce) can tomato sauce

3 large red bell peppers, halved lengthwise and seeded

1 cup shredded mozzarella cheese (dairy or plant-based)

1. Select the **SAUTÉ** setting on the Instant Pot and heat the olive oil and garlic. Add the onion and sauté until it begins to soften, about 3 minutes.

2. Add the ground beef, Italian seasoning, salt, and pepper. Sauté for about 5 minutes, or until no trace of pink remains, breaking up the meat with a spatula or wooden spoon as it cooks.

3. Pour in the broth. Use a wooden spoon to scrape up any browned bits from the bottom of the pot. Sprinkle in the bulgur wheat on top in an even layer, then pour the tomato sauce on top of the bulgur, but do not stir.

4. Secure the lid and set the pressure release to **Sealing**. Select the **PRESSURE COOK** or **MANUAL** setting for 5 minutes at high pressure. (The pot will take about 10 minutes to come up to pressure before the cooking program begins.)

5. When the cooking program ends, let the pressure release naturally for 5 minutes, then move the pressure release to **Venting** to release any remaining steam. Open the pot and stir the filling.

(Continued)

6. Preheat the air fryer to **BAKE** at 350°F and set the cooking time for 10 minutes. If using a toaster oven–style air fryer, line the cooking pan with parchment paper or aluminum foil.

7. Stuff the bell pepper halves with the bulgur-beef filling and place them on the lined pan or, if using a basket-style air fryer, in the air frying basket. Sprinkle the cheese on top of the peppers.

8. Bake the peppers in the preheated air fryer.

9. Use a spatula or tongs to transfer the peppers to plates and serve right away.

Dairy-Free (if modified), Gluten-Free   PREP TIME: **15 MINUTES**   COOK TIME: **40 MINUTES**   YIELD: **6 SERVINGS**

Buffalo Chicken–Stuffed Baked Potatoes

Baked potatoes develop wonderfully crispy, seasoned skins in the air fryer, while their topping of Buffalo chicken cooks in the Instant Pot. After a final broiling step in the air fryer to melt the cheese on top, dinner is served. If you prefer your stuffed potatoes with less heat and more sweet, try the BBQ variation in the recipe note on page 143.

POTATOES

2 teaspoons extra-virgin olive oil

6 (6-ounce) russet potatoes, well scrubbed

½ teaspoon kosher salt

¼ teaspoon freshly ground black pepper

CHICKEN

1 cup water

1 teaspoon kosher salt

2 pounds boneless, skinless chicken breasts

4 tablespoons unsalted butter (dairy or plant-based), cut into 1-tablespoon pats

4 garlic cloves, minced or pressed

½ cup Frank's RedHot sauce (not wing sauce)

2 tablespoons honey

2 teaspoons Worcestershire sauce

1. **Prepare the potatoes:** Preheat the air fryer on **BAKE** at 400°F and set the cooking time for 35 minutes. If using a toaster oven–style air fryer, line the cooking pan with parchment paper or aluminum foil.

2. In a mixing bowl, drizzle the olive oil over the potatoes, then sprinkle on the salt and pepper. Use your hands to rub the oil and seasonings all over the potatoes, coating them evenly. Place the potatoes on the lined cooking pan or, if using a basket-style air fryer, in the air frying basket.

3. Bake the potatoes in the preheated air fryer.

4. **While the potatoes are baking, make the chicken:** Add the water, salt, and chicken breasts to the Instant Pot, arranging the chicken in a single layer.

5. Secure the lid and set the pressure release to **Sealing**. Select the **PRESSURE COOK** or **MANUAL** setting for 15 minutes at high pressure. (The pot will take about 10 minutes to come up to pressure before the cooking program begins.)

(Continued)

1½ cups shredded cheddar or Monterey Jack cheese (dairy or plant-based)

¾ cup sour cream (dairy or plant-based)

½ cup sliced green onions

NOTES: If you are able to weigh your potatoes, that will help you judge the cooking time for smaller or larger ones than indicated in the recipe. My rule of thumb is as follows: 4-ounce russet potatoes take 25 minutes to cook through on the **BAKE** setting at 400°F. For every additional ounce of weight per potato, add another 5 minutes to the cooking time. This timing works for potatoes up to 8 ounces in size.

For a tasty BBQ variation, substitute ¾ cup barbecue sauce (page 165) for the Frank's RedHot, reduce the butter to 2 tablespoons, and omit the honey and Worcestershire sauce.

6. When the Instant Pot cooking program ends, perform a quick pressure release by moving the pressure release to **Venting**. Open the pot and use a pair of tongs to transfer the chicken to a cutting board or dish. Wearing heat-resistant mitts, remove the inner pot from the housing, pour out the cooking liquid (you can save it and use it as chicken broth for another recipe, or discard it), then return the pot to its housing. Turn off the pot.

7. Use a pair of forks to shred the chicken.

8. Select the **SAUTÉ** setting on the Instant Pot and melt the butter with the garlic. Sauté until the garlic is bubbling but not browned, about 2 minutes. Add the hot sauce, honey, and Worcestershire and stir to combine and let the honey melt into the other ingredients.

9. Stir in the shredded chicken, coating it with the sauce. Turn off the pot. Taste for seasoning, adding more hot sauce if needed.

10. When the air fryer cooking program ends, remove the potatoes from the air fryer. Make lengthwise and crosswise cuts in the potatoes, then use your hands to push in and up on the ends of the potatoes to split them open. Top the potatoes with the buffalo chicken and cheese.

11. Return the potatoes to the air fryer. Cook them on the **BROIL** setting at its highest temperature (some will go up to 450°F, while others top out at 400°F) for 3 minutes, until the cheese is melted and bubbly.

12. Use a spatula or tongs to transfer the potatoes to serving plates, top each one with a dollop of sour cream and a sprinkle with green onions, and serve right away.

CHAPTER 6

MAIN DISHES

Coconut Chicken Adobo

Here's a super-fast, weeknight-friendly take on Filipino-style chicken adobo. Salty soy sauce, tangy vinegar, and creamy coconut milk combine for a flavorful sauce that requires no marinating time. Serve with steamed rice (see the recipe note on page 148 for a pot-in-pot option) or Roasted Vegetables with Olive Oil and Garlic (page 218).

1½ pounds boneless, skinless chicken thighs

1 medium yellow onion, sliced

4 garlic cloves, chopped

⅓ cup soy sauce or tamari

3 tablespoons white vinegar or coconut vinegar

1 tablespoon brown sugar

1 teaspoon black peppercorns

3 bay leaves

½ cup coconut milk

Thinly sliced green onions, for garnish

1. Add the chicken, onion, garlic, soy sauce, vinegar, brown sugar, peppercorns, and bay leaves to the Instant Pot. Use a spoon or your hands to mix everything together until evenly combined.

2. Secure the lid and set the pressure release to **Sealing**. Select the **PRESSURE COOK** or **MANUAL** setting for 15 minutes at high pressure. (It will take about 10 minutes for the pot to come up to pressure before the cooking program begins.)

3. When the cooking program ends, let the pressure release naturally for at least 10 minutes, then move the pressure release to **Venting** to release any remaining steam.

4. Open the pot and add the coconut milk. Press **Cancel** to reset the cooking program, then select the **SAUTÉ** setting. Let the adobo simmer for about 10 minutes, stirring occasionally, until the sauce has thickened a bit and become a little glossy in appearance. Turn off the pot. Remove and discard the bay leaves. If you like, at this point, you can either leave the chicken thighs whole or use two forks to break them up into bite-size shreds.

(Continued)

5. Spoon the chicken and sauce onto serving plates. Sprinkle green onions on top and serve right away.

NOTE: For pot-in-pot rice, combine 1½ cups long-grain white rice or quick-cooking brown rice, 1½ cups water, and ¼ teaspoon kosher salt in a 1½-quart stainless-steel bowl. Place a raised metal steam rack in the pot after mixing up the chicken and other ingredients, then place the bowl of rice on top. The pot will take about 10 minutes longer to come to pressure.

Crispy Cornflake Chicken or Tofu Tenders

In this recipe, fast-cooking chicken tenders get the classic, nostalgic, oh-so-crispy coating of cornflakes. Serve your tenders with a simple green salad on the side or, one of my go-tos, veggies cooked from frozen in the microwave and seasoned with garlic salt and a knob of butter. Look to the recipe note on page 150 for a vegan variation using tofu.

2 large eggs

½ cup buttermilk or milk (dairy or plant-based)

1 tablespoon Frank's RedHot or Crystal hot sauce

2 cups cornflakes cereal

1 cup all-purpose flour or gluten-free flour blend

1½ teaspoons seasoned salt

½ teaspoon freshly ground black pepper

½ teaspoon poultry seasoning

½ teaspoon garlic powder

¼ teaspoon cayenne pepper

1½ pounds chicken tenders

5 tablespoons butter (dairy or plant-based), melted

Avocado oil, for spraying

1. If using a toaster oven–style air fryer, line the cooking pan with parchment paper.

2. Create a breading station with two shallow bowls. In the first bowl, whisk the eggs, buttermilk, and hot sauce until no streaks of yolk remain. In the second bowl, use your hands to crush the cornflakes into fine crumbs, then add the flour, seasoned salt, pepper, poultry seasoning, garlic powder, and cayenne and stir until evenly combined.

3. Skewer a chicken tender on a fork and dip it into the egg mixture. Wait a few seconds for the excess egg mixture to drip back into the bowl, then transfer the tender to the bowl with the cornflake mixture, pressing in the crumbs to coat it evenly. Transfer the coated chicken tender to the lined cooking pan, or to a plate if using a basket-style air fryer. Repeat with the remaining chicken tenders.

4. Preheat the air fryer on **BAKE** at 400°F and set the cooking time for 12 minutes if using a toaster oven–style air fryer, or 10 minutes if using a basket-style air fryer.

(Continued)

NOTE: For a vegetarian version, substitute 2 (14-ounce) blocks firm tofu for the chicken tenders. Use a tofu press, or wrap the tofu blocks in paper towels, place them on a plate, then place something heavy on top of the tofu, such as a heavy skillet, for 15 minutes. Cut each block of tofu crosswise into 6 planks, then proceed with the recipe as written.

5. Place the cooking pan in the air fryer, or if using a basket-style air fryer, place the coated tenders in the basket. Drizzle the butter evenly over the chicken tenders. If there are any dry, floury spots, give them a quick spritz of avocado oil.

6. Bake the chicken tenders in the preheated air fryer.

7. Use a spatula or tongs to transfer the chicken tenders to serving plates. Serve right away.

Greek Herbed Chicken Meatballs with Tzatziki Dip

These moist chicken meatballs are seasoned with oregano, mint, and lemon pepper for a Greek-inspired flavor. They're coated in panko breadcrumbs before baking, so they are crispy on the outside and juicy on the inside. Enjoy them for dinner with orzo pilaf or rice, on top of a salad using the tzatziki as a dressing, tucked into pitas or Chickpea Flatbread (page 192) with a few leaves of romaine lettuce, or as appetizers with the tzatziki alongside for dipping.

Extra-virgin olive oil, for spraying

MEATBALLS

1 pound ground chicken
(96% lean) or plant-based chicken grinds

1 large egg

¼ cup panko breadcrumbs

1 teaspoon dried oregano

1 tablespoon chopped fresh mint
or 1 teaspoon dried

1 teaspoon lemon pepper

½ teaspoon kosher salt

½ teaspoon garlic powder

¼ teaspoon freshly ground black pepper

⅛ teaspoon ground nutmeg

BREADING

1 cup panko breadcrumbs

1 teaspoon dried oregano

1 teaspoon lemon pepper

1. If using a toaster oven–style air fryer, line the cooking pan with parchment paper and spray lightly with olive oil.

2. **Prepare the meat mixture:** In a mixing bowl, combine the ground chicken, egg, panko, and seasonings. Use your hands to mix until evenly combined.

3. **Make the meatballs:** Add the panko, oregano, and lemon pepper to a shallow bowl.

4. Use a 1½-tablespoon cookie scoop to transfer a scoop of the meat mixture into the bowl of seasoned panko. Use your hands to gently toss the meatball in the breadcrumbs until it is coated all over, then transfer it to the lined cooking pan, or to a plate if using a basket-style air fryer. Repeat with the rest of the mixture.

5. Preheat the air fryer on **BAKE** at 400°F and set the cooking time for 10 minutes.

(Continued)

TZATZIKI

1 cup Greek or whole-milk yogurt
(page 10)

1 Persian cucumber, finely diced

1 tablespoon chopped fresh mint

1 garlic clove, minced or pressed

½ teaspoon kosher salt

6. Spray the meatballs lightly with olive oil, then bake them in the preheated air fryer.

7. **While the meatballs are cooking, make the tzatziki:** In a bowl, stir together the yogurt, cucumber, mint, garlic, and salt.

8. When the cooking program ends, transfer the meatballs to serving plates or bowls. Serve right away, with the tzatziki on the side.

Dairy-Free (if modified),
Gluten-Free (if modified),
Vegan (if modified)

PREP TIME: **10 MINUTES**   COOK TIME: **12 MINUTES**   YIELD: **6 BURGERS**

Masala Turkey Burgers

Juicy, flavorful turkey burgers are seasoned with garam masala for an Indian-inspired flavor. With some mixed veggies incorporated into the burgers, they're a nutritious meal in patty form. You can turn them into cheeseburgers if you like, or instead top them with sliced avocado. Air fry some store-bought fries or tots while you're putting the burgers together, if you like.

BURGERS

1 pound ground turkey (97% lean) or plant-based chicken grinds

1 (6-ounce) bag frozen mixed vegetables, thawed according to package instructions

¼ cup Greek yogurt (dairy or plant-based)

⅓ cup panko breadcrumbs (gluten-free if preferred)

¼ cup chopped fresh cilantro

1 jalapeño chile, seeded and minced (optional)

1 garlic clove, minced or pressed

1½ tablespoons tomato paste

2 teaspoons garam masala

¾ teaspoon kosher salt

Avocado oil, for spraying

1. If using a toaster oven–style air fryer, line the cooking pan with parchment.

2. Add the turkey, vegetables, yogurt, panko, cilantro, jalapeño (if using), garlic, tomato paste, garam masala, and salt to a large mixing bowl. Use your hands to mix the ingredients until evenly combined. Measure out 6 (½-cup) portions of the burger mixture, then shape them into patties, 4 inches in diameter. Place the patties on the lined cooking pan, or on a plate if using a basket-style air fryer. Spray them lightly with avocado oil.

3. Preheat the air fryer to 350°F on **BAKE** and set the cooking time for 12 minutes.

4. Place the cooking pan in the air fryer or, if using a basket-style air fryer, place the patties in the basket. Bake the burgers in the preheated air fryer.

5. When the cooking program ends, remove the burgers from the air fryer and place a slice of cheese on top of each one, if desired.

(Continued)

6 slices American cheese (optional)

6 whole-wheat or sesame hamburger buns (gluten-free if preferred)

6 tablespoons mayonnaise or Sambal Mayo (page 230)

6 tablespoons ketchup

6 green lettuce leaves

1 large tomato, thinly sliced

1 red onion, thinly sliced

Pickled jalapeño chile slices (optional)

6. Spread the burger buns with the mayo and ketchup. Place a burger on each bun and top with the lettuce, tomato, onion, and pickled jalapeños (if using). Serve right away.

Ground Beef Bulgogi and Rice

This dish has all of the savory and sweet flavors of long-marinated bulgogi beef without the long marinade. You'll simply blend the sauce, brown ground beef (or plant-based grinds) in the Instant Pot, then pour in the sauce and cook under pressure, with some white rice in a bowl right on top. Serve the beef and rice in lettuce wraps, or look to the recipe note on page 160 for spring roll and rice bowl variations.

RICE

1 cup water

1 cup long-grain white rice

BEEF AND SAUCE

½ cup water

1 kiwi or ½ ripe pear, peeled and quartered

2 garlic cloves, peeled

2 tablespoons soy sauce or tamari

2 tablespoons golden brown sugar

1 tablespoon mirin

1½ teaspoons toasted sesame oil

½ teaspoon freshly ground black pepper

1 pound ground beef (90% or leaner) or plant-based beef grinds

FOR SERVING

1 head butter lettuce, separated into leaves

1 green onion, thinly sliced

1. **Prepare the rice:** In a 1½-quart stainless-steel bowl, combine the water and rice. Set aside.

2. **Make the sauce:** In a blender, combine the water, kiwi, garlic, soy sauce, brown sugar, mirin, sesame oil, and pepper. Blend at high speed for about 30 seconds, until smooth.

3. Select the **SAUTÉ** setting on the Instant Pot. When it has preheated, add the beef and sauté for about 5 minutes, breaking it up with a wooden spoon as it cooks, until no traces of pink remain. Stir in the sauce.

4. Place a raised metal steam rack in the pot, then place the bowl of rice on the rack.

5. Secure the lid and set the pressure release to **Sealing**. Press the **Cancel** button to reset the cooking program, then select the **PRESSURE COOK** or **MANUAL** setting for 10 minutes at high pressure. (The pot will take about 5 minutes to come up to pressure before the cooking program begins.)

(Continued)

NOTES: To make this a one-pot meal, after the rice and beef mixture are cooked, stir a 1-pound bag of thawed frozen mixed vegetables into the beef, before cooking down any extra liquid on the **SAUTÉ** setting. Serve the beef and vegetable mixture in bowls, over the rice.

You can also cook this recipe without the bowl of rice, then use the ground beef mixture to make bulgogi rice paper rolls. You'll need 12 rice paper wrappers, 3 cups shredded iceberg lettuce, 1½ cups julienned carrot, and 4 green onions, thinly sliced. Dip each sheet of rice paper in warm water, place it on a work surface, and top it with ¼ cup lettuce, 3 tablespoons carrot, ¼ cup ground beef mixture, and a sprinkle of green onions. Tuck in the bottom and sides and wrap tightly. Repeat to wrap up all of the rolls, then serve right away, with sriracha sauce on the side.

6. When the cooking program ends, let the pressure release naturally for 10 minutes, then move the pressure release to **Venting**.

7. Open the pot. Wearing heat-resistant mitts, remove the bowl of rice and the steam rack.

8. Stir the ground beef. If there is still a good amount of liquid in the pot, select the **SAUTÉ** setting and let the liquid reduce for about 5 minutes or until mostly evaporated, stirring occasionally. Turn off the pot.

9. Fluff the rice with a fork. Spoon the rice and ground beef mixture onto lettuce leaves, garnish with sliced green onion, and serve right away.

Dairy-Free (if modified), Gluten-Free (if modified), Vegan (if modified)

PREP TIME: **10 MINUTES** COOK TIME: **35 MINUTES** YIELD: **4 SERVINGS**

Italian-Style Meatballs with Raisins and Pine Nuts

We eat a lot of meatballs in marinara sauce in my house, so it's nice to switch things up sometimes and add a few extra ingredients to the mix. Raisins and pine nuts bring a Sicilian-inspired flair to the meatballs, and they cook under pressure in store-bought marinara for a very easy dinner. While the meatballs cook, boil some pasta, gnocchi, or polenta to serve alongside.

1 pound ground beef (90% or leaner) or plant-based beef grinds

½ cup panko breadcrumbs

¼ cup grated or shredded parmesan cheese (optional)

¼ cup raisins or currants

2 garlic cloves, minced or pressed

3 tablespoons chopped fresh basil or parsley, plus more for serving

3 tablespoons toasted pine nuts

¾ teaspoon kosher salt

¼ teaspoon ground black pepper

½ (28-ounce) jar marinara or other tomato-based pasta sauce

½ cup water

½ teaspoon red pepper flakes (optional)

Cooked pasta, gnocchi, or polenta (gluten-free if preferred), for serving

1. In a mixing bowl, combine the ground beef, panko, parmesan (if using), raisins, garlic, basil, pine nuts, salt, and pepper. Use your hands to mix until evenly combined, then roll the mixture into 12 meatballs about the size of golf balls.

2. Select the **SAUTÉ** setting on the Instant Pot and add the marinara, water, and red pepper flakes (if using). Cook for about 3 minutes, stirring occasionally, until the sauce begins to simmer.

3. Gently drop the meatballs into the sauce in a single layer. Spoon a little bit of the marinara sauce over each meatball.

4. Secure the lid and set the pressure release to **Sealing**. Select the **PRESSURE COOK** or **MANUAL** setting for 15 minutes at high pressure. (The pot will take about 5 minutes to come up to pressure before the cooking program begins.)

(Continued)

5. When the cooking program ends, let the pressure release naturally for 10 minutes, then move the pressure release to **Venting** to release any remaining steam.

6. Portion out the pasta. Open the pot. Transfer the meatballs and sauce on top of the pasta. Sprinkle with more basil and serve right away.

BBQ Tempeh or Tofu

I have wowed vegans and omnivores alike with these delicious, plant-based stand-ins for barbecued ribs. Strips of tempeh or tofu are coated in a smoky spice rub, air-fried until they're crispy on the outside, then glazed in barbecue sauce. Make your own spice rub and barbecue sauce as written here, or use store-bought versions for an even simpler option. Serve with Golden Buttery Mash (page 233) and coleslaw for a comforting BBQ meal, or on top of a salad for lunch.

SPICE RUB

½ cup brown sugar

2 tablespoons chili powder

1 tablespoon smoked paprika

2 teaspoons ground cumin

2 teaspoons dried thyme

2 teaspoons ground mustard

2 teaspoons kosher salt

1 teaspoon garlic powder

1 teaspoon onion powder

1 teaspoon dried oregano

1 teaspoon freshly ground black pepper

(Ingredients continued)

1. **Make the spice rub:** In a bowl, stir together all of the ingredients until evenly combined. The spice rub will keep in a tightly lidded container in the pantry for up to 1 year.

2. **Make the sauce:** Combine all of the ingredients in a 1½-quart saucepan on the stove over medium heat, or in an Instant Pot on the **SAUTÉ** setting. Bring up to a simmer, then turn the heat down to low and simmer for 5 minutes, stirring often. Use the barbecue sauce right away, or transfer to a tightly lidded container and refrigerate for up to 1 month. (I actually like it best after a day or two, when the flavors have had a chance to mellow and meld.)

3. **Make the tempeh:** Cut the block of tempeh or tofu vertically into 6 pieces. Cut each piece in half—vertically once more if you're using tofu, or horizontally if you're using tempeh, to make 12 pieces.

4. Preheat the air fryer on **BAKE** at 400°F and set the cooking time for 12 minutes. If using a toaster oven–style air fryer, line the cooking pan with parchment paper.

(Continued)

BARBECUE SAUCE

⅔ cup ketchup

½ cup honey or agave nectar

⅓ cup apple cider vinegar

2 tablespoons prepared yellow mustard

1 tablespoon molasses

1½ teaspoons seasoned salt

1 teaspoon Worcestershire sauce (gluten-free if preferred)

½ teaspoon liquid smoke

½ teaspoon garlic powder

¼ teaspoon freshly ground black pepper

⅛ teaspoon cayenne pepper (optional)

TEMPEH OR TOFU

12 ounces tempeh or pressed tofu (see note)

1 tablespoon avocado oil

5. Place the tempeh on the lined cooking pan, or on a plate if using a basket-style air fryer. Drizzle the tempeh with half the avocado oil, then use your fingers to spread it out to evenly coat the tempeh. Flip the tempeh and drizzle/spread on the rest of the oil. Next, sprinkle on and rub in 1½ teaspoons of the spice rub, flip the tempeh over, then sprinkle on and rub in another 1½ teaspoons spice rub.

6. Place the cooking pan in the air fryer or, if using a basket-style air fryer, place the tempeh in the basket.

7. Bake the tempeh in the preheated air fryer. When the **Turn food** notice comes on (or two-thirds of the way through the cooking time), remove the tempeh from the air fryer. Use a pastry brush to dab on 2 tablespoons of the barbecue sauce, use a spatula to flip the tempeh, then brush on another 2 tablespoons barbecue sauce. Return the tempeh to the air fryer for the remainder of the cooking time.

8. Transfer the tempeh to serving plates. Serve warm.

NOTES: To press the tofu, use a tofu press, or wrap the tofu in paper towels, place it on a plate, then place something heavy on top of the tofu, such as a heavy skillet, for 15 minutes. Cut the tofu crosswise into 6 planks, then cut each plank in half to make 12 "ribs."

Some people like to steam their tempeh before cooking for a softer texture. Pour 1 cup water into the Instant Pot. Place a steamer basket in the pot and add the sliced tempeh to the basket. Select the **PRESSURE COOK** or **MANUAL** setting for 3 minutes at high pressure. When the cooking program ends, perform a quick pressure release by moving the pressure release to **Venting**, open the pot, and transfer the tempeh to the lined cooking pan. Spread the avocado oil on the tempeh, season with the rub, and continue with the recipe as written.

Veggie Meatloaf Muffins

Dairy Free, Gluten-Free, Vegan (if modified), Vegetarian   PREP TIME: **10 MINUTES**   COOK TIME: **25 MINUTES**   YIELD: **9 MUFFINS**

I tasted my first genuinely delicious vegetarian meatloaf (aka "neatloaf") at Ananda Fuara restaurant in San Francisco. These muffins are inspired by their delicious loaf but made vegan, dairy-free, and gluten-free. I love the small portion size and fast cook time of muffins—one is a good serving for a kiddo, while two are enough for most adults. Serve them with Golden Buttery Mash (page 233) or Steamed Vegetables with Butter and Parmesan (page 217) for a comforting dinner.

2 tablespoons extra-virgin olive oil

1 garlic clove, minced or pressed

1 small or ½ medium yellow onion, minced

½ teaspoon kosher salt

½ (14-ounce) block firm tofu, mashed

½ cup cooked brown or white rice

2 large eggs *or* ½ cup plant-based egg substitute (such as Just Egg)

1 tablespoon nutritional yeast

1 teaspoon cornstarch

1 teaspoon Italian seasoning

¼ teaspoon freshly ground black pepper

3 cups puffed rice or cornflakes cereal

¼ cup ketchup

1. Select the **SAUTÉ** setting on the Instant Pot and heat the olive oil and garlic. When the garlic begins to bubble (after about 1 minute), add the onion and salt and sauté for about 4 minutes, until the onion is softened and the garlic is just beginning to brown. Turn off the pot. Wearing heat-resistant mitts, remove the inner pot from the housing.

2. Add the tofu and cooked rice to the pot and stir to combine. Stir in the eggs, nutritional yeast, cornstarch, Italian seasoning, and pepper until well combined. Fold in the cereal, stirring gently so you don't break it up too much.

3. Preheat the air fryer on **BAKE** at 325°F and set the cooking time to 20 minutes.

4. Use a cookie scoop to scoop the mixture into 9 silicone muffin cups, filling each one to the top and mounding a bit (they won't expand very much as they cook). Spread about 1½ teaspoons ketchup on top of each muffin.

(Continued)

5. If using a toaster oven–style air fryer, place the muffins on the cooking pan. If using a basket-style air fryer, place them in the air frying basket. Bake the muffins in the preheated air fryer.

6. Remove the muffins from the air fryer, let cool for 5 minutes, then unmold them onto serving plates. Serve right away.

Dairy-Free, Vegan   PREP TIME: **10 MINUTES**   COOK TIME: **35 MINUTES**   YIELD: **4 SAUSAGES**

Seitan and White Bean Chimichurri Sausages

While you can buy a variety of vegan sausages at the grocery store these days, it's more economical and often more delicious to make your own. These are easy to put together—you'll make the dough in a food processor, roll it into logs, wrap them with parchment, and steam them in the Instant Pot for just 20 minutes under pressure. Spray them with a little oil and crisp them on your air fryer's **BROIL** setting for a few minutes, then serve them in buns for a serious improvement over store-bought meatless sausages or hot dogs.

½ (15-ounce) can white beans or chickpeas, drained and rinsed, *or* ¾ cup cooked beans or chickpeas (from 6 ounces dried)

¼ cup tightly packed fresh flat-leaf parsley leaves

2 tablespoons nutritional yeast

1 tablespoon extra-virgin olive oil

1 tablespoon red wine vinegar

1½ teaspoons chopped fresh oregano *or* ½ teaspoon dried

1 teaspoon kosher salt

½ teaspoon red pepper flakes

1 cup vital wheat gluten (seitan)

¾ cup low-sodium vegetable broth

1. In a food processor, combine the beans, parsley, nutritional yeast, olive oil, vinegar, oregano, salt, and red pepper flakes. Process in about 10 pulses until fairly smooth, scraping down the sides of the container, if necessary. Add the wheat gluten and broth and pulse about 15 more times, until a cohesive ball of dough forms. (If the dough is not forming a ball, add more wheat gluten tablespoon by tablespoon, pulsing a few times to incorporate, until the dough begins to ball up in the food processor.)

2. Turn the dough out onto a work surface and divide it into 4 equal pieces. Roll a piece into a 6-inch log, then place it on an 8-inch square of parchment paper. Roll the log in the parchment, place it seam side down, and tie the ends with kitchen twine. Repeat with the remaining dough to make 3 more sausages.

(Continued)

3. Pour a cup of water into the Instant Pot and place the metal steam rack inside. Place the sausages in a single layer on the rack. Secure the lid and set the pressure release to **Sealing**, then select the **PRESSURE COOK** or **MANUAL** setting for 20 minutes at high pressure. (The pot will take about 10 minutes to come up to pressure before the cooking program begins.)

4. When the cooking program ends, let the pressure release naturally for 10 minutes, then move the pressure release to **Venting** to release any remaining steam. Wearing heat-resistant mitts, remove the steam rack and sausages. Let the sausages cool for 30 minutes, then either unwrap and use right away, or store them in a tightly lidded container in the refrigerator for up to 4 days or in the freezer for up to 3 months.

Baked Salmon with Dijon-Apricot Glaze

A simple mixture of apricot jam and Dijon mustard creates a tangy-sweet caramelized glaze on the salmon as it cooks in the air fryer. Cut the fillets into 4-ounce or 6-ounce portions, whichever suits your needs. I like to serve the salmon with an Instant Pot side dish such as Fideos and Rice (page 197) alongside. Or for less cooking, store-bought crusty bread or dinner rolls and a green salad would work nicely, too.

1 (1½-pound) salmon fillet (skin-on or skinless)

3 tablespoons apricot jam

2 tablespoons Dijon mustard

¼ teaspoon garlic powder

¼ teaspoon kosher salt

¼ teaspoon freshly ground black pepper

1. Depending on the portion size you'd like to serve, cut the salmon fillet into either four 6-ounce fillets or six 4-ounce fillets. (Alternatively, you can ask your fishmonger to do this, or use preportioned salmon fillets, thawed from frozen.)

2. In a small bowl, stir together the jam, mustard, garlic powder, salt, and pepper.

3. Preheat the air fryer on **BAKE** at 375°F and set the cooking time for 12 minutes for thin fillets, 15 minutes for medium fillets, or 18 minutes for thick fillets. (If your fillets vary in thickness and size, you can set the time for 18 minutes, then start checking for doneness after 12 minutes of cooking, and remove the fillets as they are done.) If using a toaster oven–style air fryer, line the cooking pan with parchment paper.

4. Place the salmon fillets on the lined cooking pan or, if using a basket-style air fryer, in the air frying basket. Spread the jam mixture over the top of the fillets.

5. Bake the salmon in the preheated air fryer.

(Continued)

NOTE: The recommended safe internal temperature for cooking salmon is 145°F. If you prefer your salmon a bit less well done in the middle, you may want to cook yours to just 125°F.

6. When the cooking program ends, use an instant-read thermometer to check the fish for doneness. If it is 145°F or higher in the thickest part, it is done. If it has not yet reached temperature, place it back in the air fryer for a few minutes.

7. Transfer the fish to serving plates and serve right away.

Dairy-Free, Gluten-Free, Vegan   PREP TIME: **5 MINUTES**   COOK TIME: **10 MINUTES**   YIELD: **3 TO 4 SERVINGS**

Tofu and Asparagus with Black Bean Garlic Sauce

This four-ingredient recipe makes for a super easy, I-don't-have-time-for-real-cooking sort of dinner that still has tons of flavor. Black bean garlic sauce, available in the Asian foods section of most grocery stores (and at all Chinese markets), is a miracle condiment, giving you all of the savory, salty seasoning you need for your tofu and asparagus. Start some rice cooking in the Instant Pot before you begin preparing your tofu, and everything will be ready at the same time.

1 (14-ounce) package extra-firm tofu

12 ounces asparagus spears, cut at an angle into 2-inch lengths

1½ tablespoons Chinese black bean garlic sauce (such as Lee Kum Kee)

1 tablespoon extra-virgin olive oil

3 cups cooked rice, for serving

1. Pat the tofu dry with paper towels, then cut it into bite-size cubes.

2. Add the asparagus, black bean sauce, and olive oil to a large mixing bowl. Toss to coat the asparagus. Add the tofu and gently toss until it is coated as well.

3. Preheat the air fryer on **BAKE** at 400°F and set the cooking time for 10 minutes. If using a toaster oven–style air fryer, line the cooking pan with parchment.

4. Spread out the tofu and asparagus in an even layer on the lined cooking pan or, if using a basket-style air fryer, in the air frying basket.

5. Bake in the preheated air fryer.

6. When the cooking program ends, transfer the tofu and asparagus to serving plates or bowls. Serve right away with rice.

Fish in Coconut Curry Sauce

A satisfying, Thai-inspired curry is very doable on a weeknight when you make use of store-bought curry paste and cook fish fillets straight from the freezer. I like to use mahi mahi when we're in the mood for a firmer, meatier fish or cod for a lighter and flakier option. Serve the fish with cooked rice or cauliflower rice alongside.

1 tablespoon coconut oil or avocado oil

½ medium yellow onion, diced

1 jalapeño chile, seeded and diced (optional)

1 cup coconut milk, divided

2 tablespoons yellow or red curry paste (see note)

¾ cup water

1 pound (1-inch-thick) frozen fish fillets (mahi mahi, cod, haddock, etc.)

2 Roma or plum tomatoes, diced, *or* ¾ cup (½ [15-ounce] can) petite diced tomatoes and their liquid

FOR SERVING

1 lime, cut into wedges

3 cups cooked rice or cauliflower rice

Fresh Thai basil leaves (optional)

1 Fresno or jalapeño chile, thinly sliced (optional)

1. Select the **SAUTÉ** setting on the Instant Pot and heat the coconut oil for 2 minutes. Add the onion and jalapeño (if using) and sauté for 4 minutes, until softened and translucent and beginning to brown just a bit. Add ½ cup of the coconut milk and the curry paste and sauté for 1 minute more, until bubbling and fragrant. Turn off the pot, then stir in the water.

2. Add the fish fillets in as even a layer as you can—it's okay if they overlap a bit. Pour the tomatoes on top of the fish, but do not stir them in.

3. Secure the lid and set the pressure release to **Sealing**. Select the **PRESSURE COOK** or **MANUAL** setting for 5 minutes at high pressure. (The pot will take about 10 minutes to come up to pressure before the cooking program begins.)

4. When the cooking program ends, let the pressure release naturally for at least 10 minutes, then move the pressure release to **Venting** to release any remaining steam. Open the pot and stir in the remaining ½ cup coconut milk, taking care not to break up the fish too much.

NOTE: Mae Ploy and Aroy-D brands of curry paste pack a concentrated, spicy punch, while Thai Kitchen is much milder in flavor. If using Thai Kitchen brand, increase the amount of curry paste to ¼ cup.

5. At this point, you can either serve the dish as is, with a brothy sauce, or for a thicker sauce, transfer the fish to a serving dish, then reduce the sauce on the **SAUTÉ** setting for 10 to 15 minutes, stirring often.

6. Transfer the fish to shallow serving bowls, then spoon the sauce over the fish. Serve piping hot, with lime wedge and rice on the side, and the basil leaves and chile sprinkled on top, if you like.

CHAPTER 7

BREADS, GRAINS & PASTA

Buttermilk Drop Biscuits with Honey Butter

These tangy, tender biscuits come out with craggy tops and fluffy interiors. Spread them with honey butter for a wonderfully salty-sweet combination of flavors, or just make the biscuits to serve on their own. Pair them with just about any soup, chili, or stew.

BISCUITS

1 cup all-purpose flour or gluten-free flour blend

1 teaspoon baking powder

½ teaspoon kosher salt

¼ teaspoon baking soda

4 tablespoons unsalted butter, chilled

½ cup buttermilk

HONEY BUTTER

3 tablespoons unsalted butter, room temperature

1 tablespoon honey

⅛ teaspoon ground cinnamon

Pinch kosher salt

1. **Make the biscuits:** In a mixing bowl, stir together the flour, baking powder, salt, and baking soda. Grate in the butter with a coarse grater, working quickly so it doesn't melt in your fingers. Stir, making sure all the butter strands are individually coated with flour.

2. Add the buttermilk and stir just until the dry ingredients are all absorbed. You'll have a sticky but fairly stiff dough.

3. Preheat the air fryer on **BAKE** at 400°F and set the cooking time for 8 minutes. If using a toaster oven–style air fryer, line the cooking pan with parchment.

4. Use a 2½-tablespoon cookie scoop to drop 6 mounds of dough onto the lined cooking pan, spacing them at least 1 inch apart. If using a basket-style air fryer, scoop the dough directly into the air frying basket.

5. Bake in the preheated air fryer.

6. **While the biscuits are baking, make the honey butter:** Stir together the butter, honey, cinnamon, and salt.

(Continued)

NOTE: If you'd like to make a larger batch of biscuits, this recipe is easily doubled. Bake a dozen biscuits at once in a toaster oven–style air fryer, or bake them in two batches if using a smaller, basket-style appliance.

7. When the cooking program ends, use a thin, flexible spatula to transfer the biscuits to a serving dish. Serve right away with the honey butter.

Dairy-Free, Gluten-Free, Vegetarian

PREP TIME: **10 MINUTES**　　COOK TIME: **10 MINUTES**　　YIELD: **10 ROLLS**

Grain-Free Dinner Rolls

When my husband and I first moved to Portland, we had a favorite paleo food cart that served up amazing grain-free dinner rolls. The food cart has since closed, but I'm happy to be able to re-create their rolls at home with just a few ingredients that we usually have in our pantry. If you're following a paleo diet (or cooking for people who do), this is a great recipe to have on hand. Look to the recipe note on page 186 for an herb and garlic variation.

1½ **cups tapioca flour**

1 **cup almond flour**

1 **teaspoon kosher salt**

1 **teaspoon baking powder**

3 **large eggs**

2 **tablespoons avocado oil**

1 **teaspoon apple cider vinegar**

1 **teaspoon sesame seeds**

1. In a medium mixing bowl, stir together the tapioca flour, almond flour, salt, and baking powder until well combined.

2. In another mixing bowl, whisk together the eggs, avocado oil, and vinegar.

3. Add the egg mixture to the flour mixture. Stir until the dry ingredients are incorporated and you have a very thick, sticky batter.

4. Preheat the air fryer on **BAKE** at 375°F and set the cooking time for 10 minutes. If using a toaster oven–style air fryer, line the cooking pan with parchment paper.

5. Use a 2½-tablespoon cookie scoop to drop 10 scoops of batter onto the lined cooking pan, at least 1 inch apart. If using a basket-style air fryer, scoop the dough directly into the air frying basket. Sprinkle the sesame seeds on top of each scoop of batter.

6. Bake the rolls in the preheated air fryer.

(Continued)

NOTE: For an herb and garlic variation, add 1 teaspoon Italian seasoning and ½ teaspoon garlic powder to the dry ingredients. Omit the sesame seeds.

7. When the cooking program ends, use a spatula or tongs to transfer the rolls to a cooling rack. Let the rolls cool for 10 minutes, then enjoy them warm, or let them cool to room temperature and store in a tightly lidded container in the refrigerator for up to 1 week. Split and toast the rolls before serving.

Focaccia with Zucchini and Cherry Tomatoes

Fluffy on the inside and crispy on the outside, this olive oil–doused focaccia is one of my favorite breads to make. Topped with tomatoes, zucchini, and fresh oregano, it's a great starter during the summertime. The dough gets a 12- to 24-hour rise in the fridge, which gives it great flavor and an open crumb. Look to the recipe note on page 188 for a winter variation with potatoes and rosemary.

DOUGH

2 cups all-purpose flour

1 teaspoon instant yeast (preferably SAF)

1 teaspoon kosher salt

¾ cup plus 2 tablespoons water, room temperature

2 tablespoons extra-virgin olive oil

TOPPINGS

2 tablespoons extra-virgin olive oil, divided

½ cup halved cherry or grape tomatoes

½ cup sliced zucchini (½ medium zucchini)

Leaves from 1 oregano or thyme sprig

¼ teaspoon flaky sea salt

Freshly ground black pepper

1. In a mixing bowl, stir together the flour, yeast, and salt. Add the water and olive oil. Use a spoon or a dough whisk to mix everything together into a fairly wet, shaggy dough. Cover the bowl tightly with a reusable lid or plastic wrap, then refrigerate for 12 to 24 hours.

2. When ready to bake, spread 1 tablespoon of the olive oil in an 8-inch metal baking pan (see note) or in a quarter sheet pan if you'd like a thinner, crispier focaccia. Get a little olive oil on your fingers, then use your fingertips to spread out the focaccia dough in the pan, stretching the dough all the way to the edges of the pan. You may need to let the dough rest for a few minutes in between stretches, until it yields and conforms to the pan.

3. Preheat the air fryer on **BAKE** at 360°F and set the cooking time for 20 minutes.

(Continued)

NOTES: If you are using a basket-style air fryer (6-quart size), use an 8-inch round metal cake pan. For a toaster oven–style air fryer, use an 8-inch round or square cake pan, or a quarter sheet pan if you prefer a thinner focaccia.

For a winter variation, top the focaccia with 1 tablespoon olive oil as directed, then add a layer of thinly sliced yellow potatoes (I use 4 petite ones with the thinnest setting on my mandoline), 1 teaspoon chopped fresh rosemary, ¼ teaspoon flaky salt, and a few grinds of black pepper, then drizzle with the remaining 1 tablespoon olive oil.

4. Use your fingertips to poke dimples all over the dough. Top the dough with the tomatoes and zucchini in a single layer, then sprinkle on the oregano, salt, and a few grinds of pepper. Drizzle with the remaining 1 tablespoon olive oil.

5. Bake the focaccia in the preheated air fryer.

6. When the cooking program ends, remove the focaccia from the air fryer, let it cool in the pan or basket for 5 minutes, then use a spatula to carefully transfer it to a cooling rack. Cool to room temperature (about 30 minutes), slice into 4 large pieces or 6 smaller ones, and serve. You can also eat the focaccia while it's still warm, if you like.

Two-Ingredient Flatbreads

These flatbreads are so easy and fast to make, and Greek yogurt gives them an extra-nutritious protein boost. They are a tasty shortcut when you don't have time to cook a more involved recipe for pita, naan, or other flatbread. Serve them with Coconut Butter Chicken or Chickpeas (page 122) for an Indian-inspired weeknight meal, or alongside Shakshuka with Sausage (page 97) in place of or in addition to couscous.

1 cup plain Greek yogurt

1 cup self-rising flour, plus more for rolling

1 tablespoon extra-virgin olive oil, plus more for serving (optional)

Flaky salt, for serving (optional)

NOTE: If you don't have self-rising flour on hand, simply combine 1 cup all-purpose flour, 1½ teaspoons baking powder, and ½ teaspoon kosher salt.

1. In a small mixing bowl, use a silicone spatula to combine the yogurt and flour until it forms a soft, slightly sticky dough. Divide it into 4 pieces.

2. Preheat the air fryer on **BAKE** at 400°F and set the cooking time for 12 minutes. If using a toaster oven–style air fryer, line the cooking pan with parchment paper.

3. Generously flour a cutting board. Transfer the pieces of dough to the cutting board, and generously flour them as well. Use a rolling pin to roll the dough out into 5-inch rounds, making sure there is plenty of flour underneath the dough to prevent sticking. Brush the tops of the rounds of dough with the olive oil.

4. Place 2 flatbreads on the lined cooking pan, or directly in the air fryer basket if using a basket-style air fryer. Bake the flatbreads in the preheated air fryer for 6 minutes. Use a thin, flexible spatula or tongs to transfer the flatbreads to a plate, then bake the remaining 2 flatbreads for the remaining 6 minutes of baking time. When the cooking program ends, transfer them to the plate along with the first batch.

5. Drizzle the flatbreads with olive oil and sprinkle with flaky salt, if you like. Serve right away.

Chickpea Flatbread with Black Pepper and Rosemary

A dish with ancient origins in modern-day Italy, farinata (also known as socca) is a delicious chickpea flatbread that is naturally gluten-free and vegan, too. This version is topped with chopped rosemary, flaky salt, and black pepper. Serve the farinata with any Mediterranean-inspired meal, treat it like a sandwich bread, or tuck pieces between slices of focaccia bread for a carb-on-carb delight.

1¼ cups chickpea flour

1¼ cups water

1 teaspoon kosher salt

¼ teaspoon freshly ground black pepper

¼ cup extra-virgin olive oil, plus more for cooking and garnish

¼ teaspoon chopped fresh rosemary, for garnish

¼ teaspoon flaky salt, for garnish

Freshly ground black pepper, for garnish

NOTE: This recipe works best in a toaster oven–style air fryer. If you'd like to make it in a basket-style air fryer, you can bake it in two batches, using an 8-inch round metal cake pan lined with a round of parchment paper and greased with olive oil.

1. In a mixing bowl, whisk together the chickpea flour, water, salt, and pepper to make a pancake batter–like consistency. Cover and refrigerate for at least 1 hour or up to overnight.

2. When you are ready to bake the flatbread, preheat a toaster oven–style air fryer on **BAKE** at 375°F and set the cooking time for 17 minutes. Line a quarter sheet pan with parchment paper and grease it generously with olive oil. (See the note for instructions for a basket-style air fryer.)

3. Stir the olive oil into the batter, then pour the batter into the prepared sheet pan and place it on top of the air fryer cooking pan. Bake the flatbread in the preheated oven.

4. When the cooking program ends, remove the flatbread from the oven. Grasp the edges of the parchment to lift the flatbread out of the pan and transfer it to a cutting board. Sprinkle the flatbread with the rosemary, salt, and a few grinds of black pepper, and top with a drizzle of olive oil. Cut it into squares or wedges and serve right away, while it is still warm.

Mushroom Barley Risotto

This risotto is made with pearl barley, which, despite not technically being a whole grain (most of its outer hull is polished off), still packs an impressive 6 grams of fiber per serving. It's chewy, a little nutty, and pairs well with savory mushrooms and aged Gouda cheese. To go gluten-free, you can follow the recipe as written using medium-grown brown rice instead of the barley. Serve the risotto alongside some Seitan and White Bean Chimichurri Sausages (page 171) for a hearty, filling vegetarian meal.

2 tablespoons extra-virgin olive oil

2 garlic cloves, minced or pressed

¼ yellow onion, minced

8 ounces cremini mushrooms, sliced

½ teaspoon kosher salt

1 cup pearl barley

½ teaspoon Italian seasoning

½ cup dry white or red wine

3 cups low-sodium chicken or vegetable broth

¾ cup shredded aged Gouda or parmesan cheese

1. Select the **SAUTÉ** setting on the Instant Pot and heat the olive oil and garlic for about 1 minute, until the garlic is bubbling. Add the onion, mushrooms, and salt and sauté for 5 more minutes, until the mushrooms are wilted. Stir in the barley and Italian seasoning and sauté for 1 more minute.

2. Pour in the wine and cook for about 3 minutes, until the liquid has evaporated and the barley begins to sizzle. Stir in the broth, then scrape down the sides of the pot to make sure all the grains are submerged in the broth.

3. Secure the lid and set the pressure release to **Sealing**. Press the **Cancel** button to reset the cooking program, then select the **PRESSURE COOK** or **MANUAL** setting for 25 minutes at high pressure. (The pot will take about 10 minutes to come up to pressure before the cooking program begins.)

4. When the cooking program ends, let the pressure release naturally for 10 minutes, then move the pressure release to **Venting** to release any remaining steam. Open the pot and stir in the grated cheese.

5. Spoon the risotto into bowls and serve warm.

Dairy-Free (if modified),
Vegan (if modified),
Vegetarian

PREP TIME: **5 MINUTES**   COOK TIME: **30 MINUTES**   YIELD: **4 SERVINGS**

Fideos and Rice

My dad is from San Francisco, and growing up we often had Rice-A-Roni ("The San Francisco Treat") at dinnertime. As it turns out, this rice and noodle pilaf is easy to make from scratch, and starting with butter, olive oil, and fresh garlic really takes it up a notch from the boxed version. Serve it with Baked Salmon (page 173), Veggie Meatloaf Muffins (page 167), or whatever main dish you prefer.

1 tablespoon butter (dairy or plant-based)

1 tablespoon extra-virgin olive oil

2 garlic cloves, chopped

½ cup (2½ ounces) fideos (cut spaghetti)

1 cup long-grain white rice

1 teaspoon Italian seasoning

½ teaspoon kosher salt

¼ teaspoon ground turmeric

1½ cups low-sodium chicken or vegetable broth

1 tablespoon chopped fresh flat-leaf parsley

1. Select the **SAUTÉ** setting on the Instant Pot and heat the butter, olive oil, and garlic. When the butter is melted and the garlic is bubbling, after about 1 minute, add the fideos and sauté for about 2 minutes, until they are lightly browned and the garlic is toasted. Add the rice, Italian seasoning, salt, turmeric, and broth and stir to combine.

2. Secure the lid and set the pressure release to **Sealing**. Press the **Cancel** button to reset the cooking program, then select the **PRESSURE COOK** or **MANUAL** setting for 10 minutes at high pressure. (The pot will take about 5 minutes to come up to pressure before the cooking program begins.)

3. When the cooking program ends, let the pressure release naturally for 10 minutes, then move the pressure release to **Venting** to release any remaining steam.

4. Open the pot and use a fork to mix and fluff the pilaf. Sprinkle the parsley on top and serve right away.

(Continued)

NOTES: For a parmesan-herb variation, after cooking, while you are fluffing the pilaf with a fork, add ¼ cup grated parmesan cheese and 1 tablespoon chopped fresh basil instead of the parsley.

If you cannot find fideos (Barilla and Goya are widely available brands), use angel hair, vermicelli, or thin spaghetti, broken into ¾-inch lengths.

To make this a grain and vegetable side dish in one, add a bag of frozen mixed vegetables, thawed according to the package directions. Stir them in after cooking, as you are fluffing the rice.

Tomato Rice

This Japanese-inspired dish is comfort food at its most simple and satisfying. Rice is cooked with a combination of soy sauce, mirin, and a sprinkle of cherry tomatoes, so it turns out savory and well seasoned, with a little sweetness for balance. Serve it with Tofu and Asparagus (page 177) or Crispy Cornflake Chicken or Tofu Tenders (page 149) for a change of pace from the usual plain pot of rice.

1 cup medium-grain white rice

1 cup plus 2 tablespoons water

1 tablespoon soy sauce or tamari

1 tablespoon mirin

1 cup cherry tomatoes

2 teaspoons extra-virgin olive oil

Freshly ground black pepper, for serving

1. Rinse the rice in a fine-mesh strainer until the water runs clear. Let the rice sit in the strainer for 10 minutes.

2. Combine the rice, water, soy sauce, and mirin in the Instant Pot. Sprinkle the tomatoes on top of the rice in an even layer.

3. Secure the lid and set the pressure release to **Sealing**. Select the **RICE** setting (the time and pressure settings will adjust automatically). (The pot will take about 10 minutes to come up to pressure before the cooking program begins.)

4. When the cooking program ends, let the pressure release naturally for 10 minutes, then move the Pressure release to **Venting** to release any remaining steam.

5. Use a wooden spoon or spatula to fold in the olive oil, breaking up the tomatoes a bit.

6. Scoop the rice into serving bowls. Top with a few grinds of black pepper and serve right away.

Dairy-Free, Vegan (if modified), Vegetarian   PREP TIME: **10 MINUTES**   COOK TIME: **15 MINUTES**   YIELD: **4 TO 6 SERVINGS**

Orzo and Chickpea Pilaf

When I lived in Palo Alto, California, one of my favorite restaurants was Kali Greek Kitchen. Their main dishes are accompanied by a delicious side of orzo, chickpeas, and rice. This is my slightly simplified take on that side dish, which I serve with Greek Herbed Chicken Meatballs (page 153), or on extra-busy nights, a store-bought rotisserie chicken. A green salad usually rounds out the meal.

2 tablespoons extra-virgin olive oil

2 garlic cloves, minced or pressed

8 ounces orzo pasta

2 cups low-sodium chicken or vegetable broth

½ teaspoon dried oregano

½ teaspoon kosher salt

¼ teaspoon freshly ground black pepper

1 (15-ounce) can chickpeas, drained and rinsed, *or* 1½ cups cooked chickpeas (from 4 ounces dried)

1 tablespoon fresh lemon juice

1. Select the **SAUTÉ** setting on the Instant Pot and heat the olive oil and garlic for about 2 minutes, until the garlic is bubbling and golden. Add the orzo and sauté for about 3 more minutes, until it is sizzling and lightly toasted. Add the broth, oregano, salt, and pepper and stir to combine. Sprinkle in the chickpeas in an even layer, but do not stir.

2. Secure the lid and set the pressure release to **Sealing**. Press **Cancel** to reset the cooking program, then select the **PRESSURE COOK** or **MANUAL** setting for 5 minutes at high pressure. (The pot will take about 5 minutes to come up to pressure before the cooking program begins.)

3. When the cooking program ends, perform a quick pressure release by moving the pressure release to **Venting**. Open the pot and add the lemon juice. Use a fork to combine the chickpeas and orzo, gently fluffing up the orzo as you mix it all up. Let the pilaf sit for 5 minutes. Taste for seasoning and add more salt if needed, then fluff once more.

4. Spoon onto serving plates and serve right away.

Hawaiian-Style Macaroni Salad

This Hawaiian-inspired macaroni salad has a simple list of ingredients. With just enough mayo to make things nice and creamy, a kick from apple cider vinegar, and chopped celery for crunch factor, it's a balanced and flavorful side dish. The leftovers keep well for a couple days, too—in fact, I think this salad gets better the longer it chills. Pair it with BBQ Tempeh or Tofu (page 165) for an easy lunch or dinner.

8 ounces elbow macaroni or cavatappi (gluten-free if preferred; see note)

2 cups water

¾ cup mayonnaise

2 tablespoons whole milk

2 tablespoons apple cider vinegar

1 teaspoon soy sauce or tamari

2 teaspoons granulated sugar

½ teaspoon freshly ground black pepper

¼ teaspoon kosher salt

2 green onions, thinly sliced

1 celery stalk, diced small

1 carrot, peeled and grated

1. Combine the macaroni and water in the Instant Pot. Secure the lid and set the pressure release to **Sealing**. Select the **PRESSURE COOK** or **MANUAL** setting for 5 minutes at high pressure. (The pot will take about 10 minutes to come up to pressure before the cooking program begins.)

2. **While the macaroni is cooking, make the dressing:** In a bowl, whisk together the mayonnaise, milk, vinegar, soy sauce, sugar, pepper, and salt.

3. When the cooking program ends, perform a quick pressure release by moving the pressure release to **Venting**.

4. Wearing heat-resistant mitts, remove the inner pot from the Instant Pot housing. Add the dressing, green onions, celery, and carrots to the pot and stir to combine. It may look like there's too much liquid at first, but it will absorb and set up as the salad cools.

5. Transfer the salad to a tightly lidded container and refrigerate for at least 2 hours before serving.

(Continued)

6. When you are ready to serve the salad, give it a stir, then taste for seasoning and add salt if needed.

NOTE: My favorite gluten-free pastas for Instant Pot cooking are the ones from Banza. Their elbow chickpea pasta holds up well with pressure cooking. Reduce the cooking time to 4 minutes, and rinse the pasta well in a colander after cooking and before adding the rest of the ingredients.

Garlic Toasted Israeli Couscous with Baby Spinach

The texture of Israeli (aka pearl) couscous is like no other pasta—the little balls are so delightfully chewy, and they stick together a bit, in the best way. My toddler can't get enough of them, and I add some spinach to up the nutrition factor on this grain side dish. Serve it with any main dish you like.

2 tablespoons extra-virgin olive oil

3 garlic cloves, thinly sliced

8 ounces Israeli (pearl) couscous

2 cups low-sodium chicken or vegetable broth

¼ teaspoon Italian seasoning

¼ teaspoon kosher salt

⅛ teaspoon freshly ground black pepper

4 cups baby spinach

NOTE: You can sub in other vegetables for the spinach, if you like. I often add 1½ cups peas or mixed vegetables, thawed from frozen.

1. Select the **SAUTÉ** setting on the Instant Pot and add the olive oil and garlic. Sauté until the garlic is bubbling and golden, about 2 minutes. Add the couscous and sauté for about 5 more minutes, until it is lightly toasted. Stir in the broth, Italian seasoning, salt, and pepper.

2. Secure the lid and set the pressure release to **Sealing**. Press **Cancel** to reset the cooking program, then select the **PRESSURE COOK** or **MANUAL** setting for 6 minutes at high pressure. (The pot will take about 5 minutes to come up to pressure before the cooking program begins.)

3. When the cooking program ends, perform a quick pressure release by moving the pressure release to **Venting**.

4. Open the pot. Add the baby spinach and stir it in for a minute or so, until the leaves begin to wilt. Let sit for 1 minute, stir again, and serve right away.

CHAPTER 8

VEGETABLE DISHES

Delicata Squash and Brussels Sprouts with Walnuts

Scalloped, striped slices of delicata squash are so pretty that they make for a vegetable dish that's holiday appropriate, yet fast and easy enough to serve on a weeknight. Maple syrup, aromatic sage, and toasty walnuts add lots of autumn flair. Serve it as a side dish, or with polenta or pasta for a vegetarian meal.

1 delicata squash, halved, seeded, and cut into ½-inch-thick rings

1 pound Brussels sprouts, halved if large

2 tablespoons extra-virgin olive oil

2 tablespoons maple syrup

Leaves from 2 sage sprigs, chopped if large

½ teaspoon kosher salt

¼ teaspoon freshly ground black pepper

½ cup raw walnut halves and pieces

1. Preheat the air fryer on **ROAST** at 350°F and set the cooking time for 20 minutes. If using a toaster oven–style air fryer, line the cooking pan with parchment paper.

2. Add the squash and Brussels sprouts to a large mixing bowl. Drizzle in the olive oil and maple syrup, then sprinkle in the sage, salt, and pepper. Toss until the vegetables are evenly coated.

3. Transfer the vegetables to the lined cooking pan or, if using a basket-style air fryer, to the air frying basket. Roast the vegetables in the preheated air fryer.

4. When there are 5 minutes left in the baking time, sprinkle the walnuts on top of the vegetables. Return to the air fryer for the rest of the cooking time.

5. When the cooking program ends, transfer the vegetables to a serving dish and serve right away.

Roasted Carrots and Cauliflower with Cashew Cream

Whenever I happen upon a vegetable dish that my toddler is into, I am so excited to come back to it again and again. This is one of those recipes. Eve loves the soft, roasted cauliflower and carrots, and the cashew cream is mellow in flavor (read: kid-friendly). We often have this with a grain dish such as Fideos and Rice (page 197) and call it dinner.

CARROTS AND CAULIFLOWER

1 pound carrots, sliced into ¼-inch rounds

1 pound cauliflower florets, cut into 1-inch pieces

1 tablespoon extra-virgin olive oil

½ teaspoon kosher salt

⅛ teaspoon freshly ground black pepper

CASHEW CREAM

¼ cup raw cashews

3 tablespoons water

2 tablespoons extra-virgin olive oil

2 tablespoons fresh lemon juice or rice vinegar

¼ teaspoon ground cumin

½ teaspoon kosher salt

FOR SERVING

¼ teaspoon ground sumac

1 tablespoon chopped fresh flat-leaf parsley or cilantro

1. **Make the carrots and cauliflower:** Preheat the air fryer on **ROAST** at 350°F and set the cooking time for 20 minutes. If using a toaster oven–style air fryer, line the cooking pan with parchment paper.

2. In a mixing bowl, combine the carrots, cauliflower, olive oil, salt, and pepper. Toss to evenly coat the vegetables.

3. Transfer the vegetables to the lined cooking pan or, if using a basket-style air fryer, to the air frying basket. Roast the vegetables in the preheated air fryer.

4. **While the vegetables are roasting, make the cashew cream:** In a small (32 ounces or smaller) blender, or in a wide-mouthed mason jar with an immersion blender, blend the cashews, water, oil, lemon juice, cumin, and salt for 1 minute on high speed, until creamy and smooth.

(Continued)

NOTE: If you want an even creamier sauce, or if you find your blender isn't chopping up the cashews finely enough, soak the cashews in boiling water for 30 minutes and drain before adding to the blender.

5. When the cooking program ends, transfer the vegetables to a serving plate. Sprinkle the sumac and parsley on top, and serve the cashew cream either drizzled on top or alongside for dipping.

Blistered Green Beans with Zucchini and Romesco

In this recipe, green beans and zucchini are air fried, so they get beautifully browned. The romesco sauce is made in the air fryer, too—you'll first bake the tomatoes and bell peppers; then toast the garlic, bread, and almonds and blend them into a zippy dipping sauce.

ROMESCO

2 Roma or plum tomatoes, halved

½ red bell pepper

6 garlic cloves, peeled

½ slice white bread or gluten-free bread, cubed

¼ cup slivered almonds

¼ cup extra-virgin olive oil

1 tablespoon red wine vinegar

½ teaspoon kosher salt

GREEN BEANS AND ZUCCHINI

8 ounces green beans, trimmed

2 medium zucchini (12 ounces), cut into ¼-inch-thick rounds

1 tablespoon extra-virgin olive oil

1 garlic clove, pressed or minced

¼ teaspoon kosher salt

⅛ teaspoon freshly ground black pepper

1. **Make the romesco sauce:** Preheat the air fryer on **BAKE** at 400°F and set the cooking time for 12 minutes. If using a toaster oven–style air fryer, line the cooking pan with parchment paper or aluminum foil.

2. Place the tomatoes and bell pepper skin side up on the lined cooking pan, or in the air frying basket if using a basket-style air fryer.

3. Bake the vegetables in the preheated air fryer. When the **Turn food** notice comes on (or two-thirds of the way through the cooking time), add the garlic and bread cubes to the pan. When there are 2 minutes left to go on the cooking time, add the slivered almonds to the pan.

4. When the cooking program ends, peel the tomatoes and the bell pepper and discard the skins (it's okay if some skin still sticks to the vegetables).

5. Transfer everything from the air fryer to a blender, and add the olive oil, vinegar, and salt. Blend on medium speed for 30 seconds or so, until the sauce is blended and creamy

(Continued)

but still has a little bit of texture. Transfer the romesco to a serving bowl.

6. **Make the green beans and zucchini:** Preheat the air fryer on **AIR FRY** at 400°F and set the cooking time for 15 minutes. Once again, if using a toaster oven–style air fryer, line the cooking pan.

7. In a large mixing bowl, toss the green beans and zucchini with the oil, garlic, salt, and pepper. Spread out the vegetables in a single layer on the lined cooking pan or in the air frying basket. Air fry the vegetables in the preheated air fryer.

8. When the cooking program ends, transfer the vegetables to a serving dish. Serve right away with the romesco for dipping.

Steamed Vegetables with Butter and Parmesan

Oftentimes, a meal requires just a simple vegetable side dish to round things out. If I'm cooking a main dish in the air fryer, I'll usually end up steaming vegetables in the Instant Pot, as in this recipe for broccoli, cauliflower, and carrots, topped simply with butter and parmesan cheese. They steam for just a minute under pressure and come out soft enough for the youngest members of a family to enjoy, but not overcooked. Look to the recipe note below for a tip on how to get your vegetables al dente if you prefer.

2 cups bite-size broccoli florets

2 cups bite-size cauliflower florets

3 carrots, peeled and sliced into ¼-inch-thick rounds

1½ tablespoons unsalted butter (dairy or plant-based), cut into small pieces

¼ teaspoon kosher salt

⅛ teaspoon freshly ground black pepper

¼ cup grated or shredded parmesan cheese (dairy or plant-based)

1 tablespoon chopped fresh flat-leaf parsley

1. Pour a cup of water into the Instant Pot and place a steamer basket inside. Add the broccoli, cauliflower, and carrots to the steamer basket.

2. Secure the lid and set the pressure release to **Sealing**. Select the **PRESSURE COOK** or **MANUAL** setting for 1 minute at high pressure. (The pot will take about 10 minutes to come to pressure before the cooking program begins.)

3. When the cooking program ends, perform a quick pressure release by moving the pressure release to **Venting**.

4. Open the pot. Transfer the vegetables to a serving bowl. Dot the vegetables with the butter pieces, then sprinkle with the salt and pepper. Toss to combine and melt the butter, then sprinkle the parmesan and parsley on top. Serve right away.

NOTE: For tender-crisp steamed vegetables, you can cancel the cooking program and release the pressure immediately after the pressure has built up and the cooking program has begun to count down. Some older models of Instant Pots can actually be set for 0 (zero) minutes of cooking time to easily do this.

Roasted Vegetables with Olive Oil and Garlic

This recipe includes two cooking times/temperatures, depending on how well cooked you like your roasted vegetables. Cauliflower, zucchini, carrots, and onion are simply flavored with lots of garlic, olive oil, and salt and pepper, so you can pair them with just about any main dish. All the better if it's something made in the Instant Pot, such as Helpful Hamburger with Chickpea Macaroni and Cheddar (page 127), so you can simultaneously roast your vegetables in the air fryer, then have everything ready at the same time.

½ small head cauliflower (8 ounces), cut into bite-size florets

1 medium-large zucchini (8 ounces), sliced into ¼-inch-thick rounds

2 large carrots, sliced into ¼-inch-thick rounds

1 medium yellow onion, cut into 1-inch pieces

2 tablespoons extra-virgin olive oil

2 garlic cloves, minced or pressed

½ teaspoon kosher salt

⅛ teaspoon freshly ground black pepper

1. For browned, al dente vegetables, preheat the air fryer on **ROAST** at 375°F and set the cooking time for 15 minutes. For well-cooked, fork-tender vegetables, preheat the air fryer on **ROAST** at 350°F and set the cooking time for 20 minutes. If using a toaster oven–style air fryer, line the cooking pan with parchment paper.

2. Add the cauliflower, zucchini, carrots, and onion to a large mixing bowl. Add the olive oil, garlic, salt, and pepper and toss to evenly coat the vegetables. Transfer the vegetables to the lined cooking pan or, if using a basket-style air fryer, to the air frying basket.

3. Roast the vegetables in the preheated air fryer. When the **Turn food** notice comes on (or two-thirds of the way through the cooking time), give the vegetables a stir or shake.

4. When the cooking program ends, transfer the vegetables to a serving bowl or serving plates. Serve right away.

Super Duper Greens

Green vegetables are steamed until they're just cooked through, then tossed with a light, Chinese-inspired sauce. Serve them with Tofu and Asparagus (page 177) and cooked rice, or for an even easier meal, steam or air fry a bag of frozen pot stickers to enjoy with your veggies. I'm all about giving myself a break on busy weekdays, so this is one of my favorite ways to get dinner on the table, with a mix of home-cooked vegetables and a convenient, store-bought dish to go alongside.

¼ medium head green cabbage (8 ounces), cut into 1-inch pieces

1 broccoli crown (8 ounces), broken into 1-inch florets

2 small or 1 large zucchini (8 ounces), cut into ¼-inch thick rounds, or 8 ounces green beans or haricots verts, trimmed

2 tablespoons water

1 tablespoon soy sauce or tamari

1 tablespoon oyster sauce or vegetarian, gluten-free oyster-flavored sauce

½ teaspoon cornstarch

¼ teaspoon ground ginger

1 tablespoon avocado oil

2 garlic cloves, minced or pressed

1. Pour a cup of water into the Instant Pot and place the steamer basket inside. Add the cabbage, broccoli, and zucchini to the steamer basket.

2. Secure the lid and set the pressure release to **Sealing**. Select the **PRESSURE COOK** or **MANUAL** setting and set the cooking time for 0 (zero) minutes at low pressure. (If your Instant Pot does not have the ability to go down to a 0 minute cook time, set it for 1 minute at low pressure. The vegetables will be a bit softer. If you'd still like to accomplish the 0 minute cook time, for less well-cooked vegetables, press **Cancel** right when the pot beeps once, rather than waiting for the 1 minute of cook time to pass.)

3. When the cooking program ends, perform a quick pressure release by moving the pressure release to **Venting**. Open the pot, remove the steamer basket from the pot, pour out the water, and return the inner pot to the housing.

4. In a small bowl, stir together the water, soy sauce, oyster sauce, cornstarch, and ground ginger.

(Continued)

5. Press **Cancel** to reset the cooking program, then select the **SAUTÉ** setting and add the avocado oil and garlic. When the garlic begins to bubble (after about 1 minute), add the soy sauce mixture to the saucepan and stir to combine. When it just begins to simmer and thicken, remove the inner pot from the housing once again.

6. Add the veggies from the steamer basket to the pot and gently toss to combine with the sauce.

7. Transfer to a serving dish and serve right away.

Roasted Red Cabbage with Bacon and Onions

Cabbage, onions, and bacon are a delicious combination when roasted together for a dish with caramelized sweetness from the vegetables and bites of savory smoky bacon all throughout. Make this and Golden Buttery Mash (page 233) as sides for a store-bought rotisserie chicken for a weeknight dinner. This recipe also works well with Brussels sprouts in place of cabbage, quartered if large or halved if on the smaller side.

½ medium red cabbage (1 pound), cored and cut into 1-inch squares

4 slices center-cut bacon, cut into ½-inch pieces

1 yellow onion, diced

¼ teaspoon kosher salt

1. Preheat the air fryer on **ROAST** at 350°F and set the cooking time for 15 minutes if using a toaster oven–style air fryer or 12 minutes if using a basket-style air fryer. If using a toaster oven–style air fryer, line the cooking pan with parchment paper or aluminum foil.

2. Spread out the cabbage on the lined cooking pan or in the air frying basket. Sprinkle the bacon, onion, and salt evenly on top of the cabbage.

3. Roast the cabbage in the preheated air fryer. When the **Turn food** notice comes on (or two-thirds of the way through the cooking time), give everything a stir to combine.

4. When the cooking program ends, transfer the cabbage to a serving dish and serve right away.

Creamed Corn with Green Chiles

Creamed corn gets a Southwestern makeover when you add diced green chiles and a topping of salty Cotija cheese. It's mild, creamy, cheesy, and delicious. You can use a bag of corn kernels straight from the freezer, so there's hardly any preparation besides chopping up an onion. Serve the corn as a side with any Tex-Mex or Mexican main dish, or with store-bought or homemade Crispy Cornflake Chicken or Tofu Tenders (page 149) cooked in the air fryer.

1 tablespoon butter or avocado oil

1 small yellow onion, diced

1 (1-pound) bag frozen corn kernels

1 (7-ounce) can diced roasted mild green chiles

½ cup low-sodium vegetable broth

½ cup shredded Mexican cheese blend

¼ cup cream cheese, room temperature

¼ teaspoon kosher salt

Pinch cayenne pepper

FOR SERVING

¼ cup crumbled Cotija cheese

1 tablespoon chopped fresh cilantro

½ teaspoon chili powder

1. Select the **SAUTÉ** setting on the Instant Pot and add the butter. When the butter has melted (after about 1 minute), add the onion. Sauté for about 3 minutes, until the onion has softened. Add the corn, green chiles, and broth and stir to combine.

2. Secure the lid and set the pressure release to **Sealing**. Press the **Cancel** button to reset the cooking program, then select the **PRESSURE COOK** or **MANUAL** setting for 2 minutes at high pressure. (The pot will take about 5 minutes to come up to pressure before the cooking program begins.)

3. When the cooking program ends, perform a quick pressure release by moving the pressure release to **Venting**. Open the pot. Add the Mexican cheese, cream cheese, salt, and cayenne and stir until well combined.

4. Ladle the corn into a serving bowl. Sprinkle the Cotija cheese, cilantro, and chili powder on top and serve right away.

Japanese-Style Potato Salad

This potato salad is a mash-up (pun intended) of Japanese and Western styles. It borrows technique from Japanese potato salads, which tend to have a more mashed consistency and include lots of vegetables, but it's on the savory side, with American-style mayonnaise, chopped dill pickles, and green onions. Serve the salad with Tempeh Sandwiches (page 39) or Masala Turkey Burgers (page 155).

1½ **pounds russet or Yukon Gold potatoes, peeled and cut into 2-inch pieces**

2 **large eggs**

1½ **cups frozen peas, carrots, and corn, thawed**

4 **green onions, thinly sliced**

1 **dill pickle, sliced into thin rounds**

½ **cup mayonnaise**

¼ **teaspoon kosher salt**

¼ **teaspoon freshly ground black pepper**

1. Pour a cup of water into the Instant Pot and place the steamer basket inside. Add the potatoes to the basket and place the eggs on top of the potatoes.

2. Select the **PRESSURE COOK** or **MANUAL** setting for 5 minutes at high pressure. (The pot will take about 10 minutes to come up to pressure before the cooking program begins.)

3. While the potatoes are cooking, prepare an ice bath for the eggs.

4. When the cooking program ends, perform a quick pressure release by moving the pressure release to **Venting**. Open the pot and transfer the eggs to the ice bath. Place the potatoes in a large mixing bowl.

5. Use a potato masher to mash the potatoes to a rustic texture—you still want some lumps.

6. Once cooled, peel and chop the eggs. Add them to the bowl with the potatoes. Add the thawed vegetables, green onions, pickle, mayo, salt, and pepper. Mix to combine. Taste for seasoning, adding more salt if needed.

7. Serve the salad right away, at room temperature, or cover and chill it in the fridge before serving, up to 3 days.

Dairy-Free (if modified), Gluten-Free, Vegan (if modified), Vegetarian

PREP TIME: **10 MINUTES**   COOK TIME: **30 MINUTES**   YIELD: **4 TO 6 SERVINGS**

Crash Hot Masala Potatoes

If you've never had a crash hot potato, you're in for a treat! They're golden and crisp on the outside and fluffy on the inside. The trick is to steam the potatoes whole in the Instant Pot, smash them and add oil and seasonings, then bake them to a crisp in the air fryer. This Indian-inspired version uses an aromatic spice blend of cumin, turmeric, and cayenne pepper. If you have it on hand, add a spoonful of chickpea flour—it helps create an even crispier crust on the potatoes. Serve with Coconut Butter Chicken or Chickpeas (page 122) for a flavorful, vegetarian meal.

1½ pounds petite/baby gold/fingerling potatoes (1½ inches in diameter or smaller)

1 tablespoon chickpea flour (optional)

¾ teaspoon kosher salt

¾ teaspoon ground cumin

¼ teaspoon ground turmeric

⅛ teaspoon cayenne pepper

2 tablespoons extra-virgin olive oil, divided

⅓ cup plain whole-milk yogurt or sour cream (dairy or plant-based), for serving

1½ tablespoons chopped fresh cilantro and/or mint, for serving

1 lime, cut into wedges, for serving

1. Pour a cup of water into the Instant Pot and place the steamer basket inside. Add the potatoes to the basket.

2. Secure the lid and set the pressure release to **Sealing**. Select the **PRESSURE COOK** or **MANUAL** setting and set the cooking time for 5 minutes at high pressure. (The pot will take about 10 minutes to come up to pressure before the cooking program begins.)

3. While the potatoes are cooking, in a small bowl, mix together the chickpea flour (if using), salt, cumin, turmeric, and cayenne.

4. When the cooking program ends, perform a quick pressure release by moving the pressure release to **Venting**.

5. Open the pot. Transfer the potatoes to a cutting board, then lightly smash each potato with the bottom of a glass so they're about ¾ inch thick. (It's fine if some of the potatoes break in half or come apart a bit.)

(Continued)

6. Preheat the air fryer on **BAKE** at 375°F and set the cooking time for 15 minutes. If using a toaster oven–style air fryer, line the cooking pan with parchment.

7. Drizzle 1 tablespoon of the olive oil over the potatoes, then sprinkle on half of the spice mixture. Flip the potatoes over gently, taking care not to break them up too much, and top with the remaining 1 tablespoon oil and spices, using your fingers to combine the oil and spices into a paste on the potatoes. Make sure they're evenly coated and no dry patches remain.

8. Transfer the potatoes, in as even a layer as possible, to the lined cooking pan or the air frying basket.

9. Bake the potatoes in the preheated air fryer. When the **Turn food** notice comes on (or two-thirds of the way through the cooking time), use a spatula to gently flip the potatoes.

10. When the cooking program ends, transfer the potatoes to a serving plate. Top with the yogurt and cilantro. Serve right away with lime wedges on the side.

Parsnip and Sweet Potato Fries with Sambal Mayo

Homemade fries get an extra boost of flavor and nutrition when you use parsnips and sweet potatoes in place of the usual russets. They're browned on the outside, soft on the inside, and perfect paired with a spicy mayonnaise for dipping. Serve them with store-bought sausages or homemade Seitan and White Bean Chimichurri Sausages (page 171) or Baked Salmon (page 173).

1 large sweet potato (12 ounces), peeled and cut into ½-inch-thick fries

1 medium parsnip (8 ounces), peeled and cut into ½-inch-thick fries

1 tablespoon extra-virgin olive oil

¼ teaspoon kosher salt

¼ cup mayonnaise or plant-based mayonnaise

1 teaspoon sambal oelek or sriracha

1. Preheat the air fryer on **AIR FRY** at 400°F and set the cooking time for 13 minutes if using a toaster oven–style air fryer or 11 minutes if using a basket-style air fryer.

2. Add the sweet potato and parsnip to a large mixing bowl. Add the olive oil and salt, then toss to coat the fries evenly. Spread out the fries in an even layer in the air frying basket.

3. Air fry the fries in the preheated air fryer. When the **Turn food** notice comes on (or two-thirds of the way through the cooking time), stir or shake the fries.

4. While the fries are cooking, mix up the mayo and sambal oelek in a small bowl.

5. Transfer the fries to serving plates. Serve warm with the mayo on the side for dipping.

Dairy-Free, (if modified), Gluten-Free, Vegan (if modified), Vegetarian

PREP TIME: **5 MINUTES**   COOK TIME: **15 MINUTES**   YIELD: **6 SERVINGS**

Golden Buttery Mash

The Instant Pot is my favorite tool for making mashed vegetables—they steam very quickly, then all that's left to do is mash and season with butter and salt. This is my favorite blend, a combination of gently sweet butternut squash and densely rich Yukon Gold potatoes. It goes well with Veggie Meatloaf Muffins (page 167), Crispy Cornflake Chicken or Tofu Tenders (page 149), and many other main dishes. It's a great holiday side, too.

1 (1¾-pound) butternut squash, peeled and cut into 1-inch cubes

3 medium Yukon Gold potatoes (about 1¼ pounds), peeled and cut into 1-inch cubes

2 tablespoons butter or plant-based butter

1 teaspoon kosher salt

1. Pour a cup of water into the Instant Pot and place the steamer basket inside. Add the squash and potatoes to the basket.

2. Secure the lid and set the pressure release to **Sealing**. Select the **PRESSURE COOK** or **MANUAL** setting for 4 minutes at high pressure. (The pot will take about 10 minutes to come to pressure before the cooking program begins.)

3. When the cooking program ends, perform a quick pressure release by moving the pressure release to **Venting**. Open the pot and, wearing heat-resistant mitts, remove the steamer basket. Lift out the inner pot, pour out the water, and return the steamed squash and potatoes to the warm pot.

4. Add the butter and salt to the pot. Use a potato masher to mash the vegetables until they are mostly smooth—it's fine if a few lumps remain. Taste for seasoning, adding more salt if needed.

5. Transfer to a serving bowl and serve right away.

CHAPTER 9

SWEET TREATS

Dairy-Free, Gluten-Free (if modified), Vegetarian (if modified)

PREP TIME: **10 MINUTES**

COOK TIME: **50 MINUTES**

YIELD: **9 LARGE BROWNIES**

Rocky Road Brownies

Brownies get an upgrade with add-ins of chocolate chips and walnuts, and a rocky road–inspired marshmallow topping. In a toaster oven–style air fryer, the marshmallows get a quick toasting on the **BROIL** setting, so they're crisp and browned on the outside and chewy in the middle (look to the recipe note for modified instructions for basket-style air fryers). Serve these with a cold glass of milk, or with vanilla ice cream and chocolate sauce for a killer brownie sundae.

Avocado oil spray

3 cups powdered sugar

¾ cup all-purpose flour or gluten-free flour blend

⅔ cup unsweetened cocoa powder

½ cup avocado oil

2 large eggs

3 tablespoons water

½ teaspoon vanilla extract

¼ teaspoon kosher salt

⅔ cup chocolate chips, divided

1 cup walnut pieces, divided

1 cup mini marshmallows (regular or plant-based)

1. Spray an 8-inch baking pan with avocado oil (see note).

2. In a mixing bowl, whisk together the powdered sugar, flour, and cocoa powder. Add the avocado oil, eggs, water, vanilla, and salt and stir to combine until the dry ingredients are absorbed. Add half of the chocolate chips and half of the walnuts and stir until evenly mixed.

3. Preheat the air fryer on **BAKE** at 300°F and set the cooking time for 45 minutes. Transfer the brownie batter to the baking pan, then sprinkle on the remaining chocolate chips and walnuts.

4. Bake the brownies in the preheated air fryer.

5. When the cooking program ends, sprinkle the marshmallows on top of the brownies. Cook the brownies on your air fryer's **BROIL** setting at its highest temperature (some will go up to 450°F, while others top out at 400°F) for 3 minutes, or just until the marshmallows are puffed and toasty brown.

6. Remove the brownies from the oven. Let them cool in the pan for at least 2 hours, then slice and serve.

(Continued)

NOTES: If you are using a basket-style air fryer (6-quart size), use an 8-inch round metal cake pan, stir all of the walnuts, chocolate chips, and marshmallows into the batter (do not reserve any for topping), and increase the cooking time to 1 hour. Skip the broiling step. The brownies will be fudgy on the inside with an extra-crispy top layer.

If you are using a toaster oven–style air fryer, you can use an 8-inch round or square metal cake pan for more evenly baked brownies, or an 8-inch square Pyrex dish for a brownie with an extra-gooey center. If you like, you can line the bottom of the cake pan with a round of parchment for easier unmolding.

For an even quicker treat, you can use a store-bought brownie mix for this recipe. Any 18- to 19-ounce boxed mix will work well—I like the classic Betty Crocker fudge brownie mix. Substitute the boxed mix for the powdered sugar, flour, and cocoa powder.

Puff Pastry Braid with Guava and Cream Cheese

A store-bought sheet of puff pastry makes for a very easy yet impressive-looking dessert when filled, braided, and baked in a toaster oven–style air fryer. This one is inspired by my friend Marta Rivera's pastelillos, with a sweetened cream cheese filling underneath the traditional guava paste. Slice and serve with coffee for dessert, or as Marta serves her pastelillos, as a morning or afternoon treat.

4 ounces cream cheese, at room temperature

2 tablespoons plus 1 teaspoon granulated sugar

1 tablespoon all-purpose flour, plus more for dusting

1 large egg, separated

½ teaspoon vanilla extract

Pinch kosher salt

1 frozen puff pastry sheet, thawed at room temperature for 40 minutes

6 (⅛-inch-thick) slices guava paste (about 4 ounces; see note)

1. In a bowl, stir together the cream cheese, 2 tablespoons of the sugar, flour, egg yolk, vanilla, and salt until evenly mixed.

2. Unfold the puff pastry on a lightly floured surface. Use a rolling pin to roll it out lengthwise, until it is about 11 inches long. Transfer the puff pastry to a sheet of parchment paper.

3. With a sharp paring knife, cut 1-inch diagonal strips, lengthwise, one-third of the way into the puff pastry on either side, leaving the middle third intact. (These dough strips will later be folded over the top of the filling in a braid.) You should end up trimming away triangle-shaped wedges at the bottom and top of the pastry.

4. Spread out the cream cheese mixture along the middle third of the pastry, leaving about 1 inch at the top and bottom of the pastry bare. Lay the strips of guava paste along the middle of the cream cheese.

(Continued)

NOTE: Guava paste (pasta de guayaba) is available in most Hispanic grocery stores and online. Iberia brand, which comes in an easily sliceable block, is my favorite one to use. You can substitute quince paste (membrillo) for the guava paste, if you like.

5. Fold the top and bottom bare inches of the pastry over onto the cream cheese filling. Then, alternating sides, fold the diagonal strips over the top of the cream cheese and guava paste, to make a braid.

6. Preheat a toaster oven–style air fryer on **BAKE** at 375°F and set the cooking time for 14 minutes. Line the cooking pan with parchment or aluminum foil.

7. Use a pastry brush to brush the egg white over the pastry braid, then sprinkle the top with the remaining 1 teaspoon sugar. Transfer the pastry braid to the lined cooking pan.

8. Bake the braid in the preheated toaster oven–style air fryer.

9. When the cooking program ends, carefully transfer the braid to a cooling rack. Allow it to cool for at least 20 minutes before serving. Transfer to a serving dish, cut into slices, and serve warm or at room temperature.

Dairy-Free (if modified),
Vegan (if modified),
Vegetarian

PREP TIME: **15 MINUTES
(PLUS 15 MINUTES TO
COOL FILLING)**

COOK TIME: **15 MINUTES**

YIELD: **20 WONTONS (4 TO
6 SERVINGS)**

Apple Pie Wontons

Use your Instant Pot or a skillet on the stove to make a quick apple pie filling, then spoon it into wonton wrappers and air fry them for an easy dessert. They're so cute and bite-size, appealing to kids and adults alike. Serve them on their own, or pile them on top of a scoop of vanilla ice cream for a sundae treat.

PIE FILLING

1 tablespoon cornstarch

1 tablespoon fresh lemon juice

3 tablespoons water

1 tablespoon unsalted butter
(dairy or plant-based)

1 large Granny Smith or other tart
apple, peeled, cored, and diced
small

¼ cup brown sugar

½ teaspoon pumpkin pie spice

Pinch kosher salt

WONTONS

20 square or round wonton or
potsticker wrappers (regular or
plant-based)

1 tablespoon cornstarch

1 tablespoon water

Avocado oil, for spraying

Vanilla ice cream, for serving
(optional)

1 tablespoon powdered sugar,
for serving

1. **Make the filling:** In a small bowl, stir together the cornstarch, lemon juice, and water.

2. Select the **SAUTÉ** setting on the Instant Pot and melt the butter (alternatively, melt the butter in a medium skillet on the stovetop over medium heat). Add the apples, brown sugar, pumpkin pie spice, and salt and sauté for about 5 minutes, until the apples are softened and cooked through.

3. Stir up the cornstarch mixture once more, then add it to the apples and cook for about 30 seconds, stirring constantly, until thickened and glossy. Turn off the pot or remove the skillet from the heat, transfer the filling to a bowl, and let it cool until it is no longer piping hot, about 15 minutes. It will be very thick.

4. **Make the wontons:** If using a toaster oven–style air fryer, line the cooking pan with parchment paper. Lay out the wonton wrappers on a work surface. In a small bowl, stir together the cornstarch and water.

(Continued)

5. Portion out a generously heaped teaspoon of the filling into the middle of a wonton wrapper. Use a pastry brush or your fingers to brush the cornstarch mixture onto the edges of the wonton wrapper. Gather up the corners of the wonton wrapper and pinch them together at the top, then pinch along the seams, to make a little four-cornered pouch. Place the wonton on the lined cooking pan or on a plate if using a basket-style air fryer. Repeat with the remaining wrappers and filling.

6. Select the **BAKE** setting at 375°F and set the cooking time for 5 minutes if using a toaster oven–style air fryer or 4 minutes if using a basket-style air fryer.

7. Spray the wontons liberally with avocado oil.

8. Bake the wontons in the preheated air fryer, on the lined cooking pan if using a toaster oven–style air fryer or in the air frying basket if using a basket-style air fryer.

9. When the cooking program ends, remove the wontons from the air fryer. Transfer the wontons to a serving platter or into serving bowls with ice cream (if you like), sprinkle with powdered sugar, and serve right away.

Vegetarian PREP TIME: **10 MINUTES (PLUS 12 HOURS TO COOL)** COOK TIME: **55 MINUTES** YIELD: **6 TO 8 SERVINGS**

Mango and Greek Yogurt Cheesecake

This cheesecake has a whole mango and some Greek yogurt blended right into the filling for a fruity, tangy, and light result. The graham cracker topping gets a hit of ginger, which pairs nicely with mango. Topped with a store-bought jam glaze, it's pretty enough to serve to company but easy enough to enjoy anytime.

CRUST

Avocado oil spray

6 graham cracker sheets

2 tablespoons brown sugar

½ teaspoon ground ginger

1½ tablespoons unsalted butter, melted

FILLING

1 (8-ounce) package cream cheese, room temperature

1 large ripe mango, pitted, peeled, and cut into chunks (about 1½ cups)

½ cup whole-milk Greek yogurt

⅓ cup honey or agave nectar

1 tablespoon all-purpose flour

1 teaspoon vanilla extract

2 large eggs, at room temperature

1. **Make the crust:** Line the base of a 7-inch springform pan with a round of parchment paper. Spray the sides of the pan and the parchment with avocado oil.

2. In a food processor, process the graham crackers to fine crumbs. Add the brown sugar, ground ginger, and melted butter and pulse until the mixture resembles damp sand.

3. Transfer the crumb mixture to the prepared pan and press firmly into an even layer on the bottom and about ½ inch up the sides. Set aside in the freezer while you make the filling.

4. **Make the filling:** In the food processor, combine the cream cheese, mango, yogurt, honey, flour, and vanilla. Process until fairly smooth, about 1 minute—it's fine if you can still see some texture from the mango, but there shouldn't be any large chunks. Add the eggs for 2 pulses each. It's fine if some streaks of egg yolk remain.

5. Pour the filling into the crust. Gently tap the pan on the counter a few times to remove some of the air bubbles. Cover the pan tightly with aluminum foil.

(Continued)

⅓ cup mango jam (or mango-pineapple, mango-peach, peach-pineapple, or another tropical fruit jam)

1 teaspoon fresh lemon juice

6. Pour a cup of water into the Instant Pot. Place the pan in a long-handled silicone sling and lower it into the pot.

7. Secure the lid and set the pressure release to **Sealing**. Select the **PRESSURE COOK** or **MANUAL** setting for 40 minutes at high pressure. (The pot will take about 10 minutes to come up to pressure before the cooking program begins.)

8. When the cooking program ends, let the pressure release naturally for 20 minutes, then move the pressure release to **Venting**.

9. Open the pot and, wearing heat-resistant mitts, grasp the handles of the sling and lift the pan out of the pot. Remove the aluminum foil, taking care not to get burned from the steam. Use a paper towel to dab off any excess moisture that may have settled on top of the cheesecake. The cake will be a bit puffed up and uneven at first, but it will settle and even out as it cools.

10. **Make the glaze:** In a small saucepan on the stovetop, or in the Instant Pot on the low **SAUTÉ** setting, heat the jam and lemon juice for 3 to 4 minutes, until it begins to simmer. Pour the glaze over the cheesecake, using a small spatula to spread it out in an even layer.

11. Leave the cheesecake to cool on the counter for 2 hours, then cover and transfer it to the fridge. Let chill for at least 10 hours, or up to 24 hours before serving. Unmold the cheesecake from the pan, then slice into wedges and serve.

Cozy Cardamom Rice Pudding

This mellow, creamy dessert is wonderfully comforting on its own and becomes a company-worthy dish when topped with vibrantly colored pistachios and pomegranate seeds. The flavors are inspired by Indian kheer, but the method and ingredients are more along the lines of an American-style rice pudding, using eggs to thicken the pudding to a creamy custard consistency.

½ cup basmati or long-grain white rice

1½ cups water

1¾ cups whole milk

½ cup granulated sugar

2 large eggs

1 teaspoon ground cardamom

¾ teaspoon kosher salt

¾ cup chopped pistachios, for serving (optional)

¾ cup pomegranate arils, for serving (optional)

1. Combine the rice and water in the Instant Pot. Secure the lid and set the pressure release to **Sealing**. Select the **RICE** setting. (The pot will take about 5 minutes to come up to pressure before the cooking program begins.)

2. While the rice is cooking, combine the milk, sugar, eggs, cardamom, and salt in a blender. Blend the mixture on low speed for about 20 seconds, until smooth. Set aside.

3. When the cooking program ends, let the pressure release naturally for 10 minutes, then move the pressure release to **Venting** to release any remaining steam.

4. Open the pot and use a whisk to break up the cooked rice. Whisking constantly, pour the mixture from the blender into the pot in a thin stream.

(Continued)

NOTES: If you like, you can substitute 1 teaspoon ground cinnamon or 1 teaspoon vanilla extract for the cardamom.

5. Press the **Cancel** button to reset the cooking program, then select the **SAUTÉ** setting. Cook the pudding for 3 to 4 minutes, whisking constantly, until it just barely begins to steam and the temperature reaches 165 to 170°F when measured with an instant-read thermometer. (The pudding will still be quite liquid at this point, but it will set as it cools. Don't cook it further, as the mixture will begin to curdle if you let it boil.) Turn off the pot.

6. Wearing heat-resistant mitts, lift the inner pot out of the Instant Pot housing. Give the pudding a final stir, then pour it into a 6-cup Pyrex or ceramic dish or into individual serving bowls or ramekins. Cover and chill the pudding in the refrigerator for at least 3 hours before serving.

7. If you chilled the pudding in a larger dish, spoon it into serving bowls. Top each serving with pistachios and pomegranate arils (if using) and serve.

Dairy-Free (if modified),
Vegan (if modified),
Vegetarian

PREP TIME: **10 MINUTES (PLUS 20 MINUTES TO COOL)**   COOK TIME: **55 MINUTES**   YIELD: **4 TO 6 SERVINGS**

Peach and Blueberry Pecan Crumble

I love that this summery crumble can be made with frozen fruit any time of year for a little hit of sunshine. Just place your frozen peaches and blueberries in the fridge the night before you want to bake the cobbler (I pour them right into the Pyrex so they're ready to go), or spread them out in an even layer on a rimmed baking sheet on the countertop about 2 hours in advance for a quicker thaw. You can, of course, use fresh peaches and blueberries (or any stone fruits and berries, for that matter) if they're in season.

PEACH FILLING

1 pound frozen sliced peaches, thawed (see headnote)

1 cup frozen blueberries, thawed

2 teaspoons fresh lemon juice

¼ cup granulated sugar

1 tablespoon cornstarch

¼ teaspoon ground cinnamon

¼ teaspoon ground ginger

CRUMB TOPPING

⅔ cup all-purpose flour

⅓ cup brown sugar

4 tablespoons unsalted butter, room temperature

¼ teaspoon ground cinnamon

¼ teaspoon ground ginger

¼ teaspoon kosher salt

½ cup pecan pieces, chopped

Vanilla ice cream, whipped cream, or Greek yogurt, for serving (optional)

1. **Prepare the filling:** Combine the peaches, blueberries, lemon juice, sugar, cornstarch, cinnamon, and ginger in an 8-inch round cake pan. Stir until evenly mixed, then spread out in an even layer.

2. **Prepare the crumb topping:** Add the flour, brown sugar, butter, cinnamon, ginger, and salt to a mixing bowl. Use a fork or pastry blender to stir until it is well combined, with a sandy/crumbly texture. Add the pecan pieces and stir to combine.

3. Preheat the air fryer on **BAKE** at 300°F and set the cooking time for 55 minutes.

4. Sprinkle the crumble topping evenly over the peaches. Bake the crumble in the preheated air fryer.

5. When the cooking program ends, remove the crumble from the air fryer and let cool for at least 20 minutes.

6. Scoop servings of the crumble into serving bowls and top with ice cream, whipped cream, or yogurt, if you like.

Pear and Cranberry Sauce

Here's a nutritious and sweet dessert or snack-time treat that both adults and kids can enjoy. Mash it for a chunkier texture, or use a blender to get it super smooth. I serve this just like I would applesauce, on its own or with a little ground cinnamon on top. It's also wonderful with latkes for Hanukkah, or as a topping for waffles or pancakes. If you've got babies or toddlers, spoon it into reusable pouches for an on-the-go option.

3 pounds ripe Anjou pears, peeled, quartered, and cored

½ cup dried cranberries

½ cup pear juice, apple juice, or water

½ teaspoon ground ginger

Ground cinnamon, for serving (optional)

NOTES: If your pears are on the firmer side, increase the cooking time to 5 minutes.

You can substitute ½ cup raisins, dried blueberries, or chopped dried apricots for the cranberries.

1. Add the pears, cranberries, juice, and ginger to the Instant Pot and stir to combine.

2. Secure the lid and set the pressure release to **Sealing**. Select the **PRESSURE COOK** or **MANUAL** setting for 3 minutes at high pressure. (The pot will take about 10 minutes to come up to pressure before the cooking program begins.)

3. When the cooking program ends, let the pressure release naturally, about 10 minutes.

4. Open the pot, pour out and discard about ½ cup of the cooking liquid, then mash with a potato masher for chunky sauce or blend with an immersion blender or regular blender for smoother sauce.

5. Serve warm or chilled, with a sprinkle of cinnamon on top, if you like. The sauce will thicken a bit as it cools.

Dairy-Free, Gluten-Free, Vegan (if modified)   PREP TIME: **5 MINUTES**   COOK TIME: **1 HOUR 10 MINUTES**   YIELD: **4 SERVINGS**

Dried Apricot Compote

When I was growing up, my mother would often make us a bowl of compote for dessert. She'd pour water over dried fruit, then leave it to soak in the refrigerator for a day or more. When you use the Instant Pot, this process speeds up considerably—in just over an hour, the fruit is soft and hydrated and has made its own light syrup. Apricots are my favorite dried fruit to use, along with a handful of dried cranberries or raisins. For a light dessert, serve the compote over plain or vanilla-flavored Greek yogurt.

1 lemon

6 ounces dried apricots (about 1¼ cups)

½ cup dried cranberries or raisins

2 cups water

Plain or vanilla Greek yogurt, for serving (optional)

NOTE: The liquid for the compote will be a bit watery at first, but it will thicken as it chills. If you prefer a thicker syrup for your compote, you can reduce the cooking liquid on the Instant Pot's **SAUTÉ** setting for about 5 minutes before serving.

1. Working over the Instant Pot, peel the lemon zest in long strips. When done, squeeze in the lemon juice. Add the apricots, cranberries, and water and stir to combine.

2. Secure the lid and set the pressure release to **Sealing**. Select the **PRESSURE COOK** or **MANUAL** setting for 1 minute at low pressure. (The pot will take about 10 minutes to come up to pressure before the cooking program begins.)

3. When the cooking program ends, let the pressure release naturally and leave the pot covered on the **Keep Warm** setting for 1 hour.

4. Open the pot and discard the lemon zest strips. Serve the compote warm or chilled, on its own or over yogurt.

ACKNOWLEDGMENTS

I am so grateful to be able to do what I love, writing cookbooks that make use of innovative kitchen technologies. To incorporate my two favorite appliances into one book has been an incredibly fun and creativity-sparking project, and so many people have helped, contributed their talents, and supported me along the way.

To my husband, in our second year in this work-from-home bubble, we've somehow managed to keep getting along, loving each other, and supporting each other in our professional pursuits, all while raising a wild and wonderful toddler *and* getting ready to welcome a second child into our family. I don't know how we're doing it all, but I'm so glad you're the partner I have on this crazy ride.

To my agent, Alison Fargis, thank you for going the extra mile on this project to coordinate photography (and all manner of other things book-related!) from your post on the East Coast. I absolutely could not have done it without your help and expertise.

To the team at HarperCollins, thank you so much for working with me to make this cookbook. Thanks to editor Deb Brody and her incredible assistant, Jacqueline Quirk, copy editor Karen Wise, art director Melissa Lotfy, designer Shubhani Sarkar, photographer Dana Gallagher, and food stylist Cyd McDowell for lending your considerable and wide-ranging talents to this project.

To Mellanie Garrett and the rest of the team at Instant Brands, thank you for supporting me in the writing of my seventh authorized cookbook. I'm always excited to see what incredible kitchen technology you produce, and it's so much fun to write recipes that make use of it.

To my head recipe tester, Heather Nelson, every recipe you've cross-tested is better for your feedback. A cookbook worth its salt needs someone like you working behind the scenes, and I'm so lucky to have you on my team.

And last but not least, thank you to my network of Portland moms. You're the main inspiration for this cookbook, after all. I wanted to create a collection of cohesive, straightforward, nutritious, and weekday-friendly recipes that we could all use to feed our families well, and I hope I've hit the mark here. You all impress me every day with your strength and perseverance raising littles and doing everything else you do.

TIME AND TEMPERATURE CHART
FOR TOASTER OVEN-STYLE AIR FRYERS

FOOD	SMART PROGRAM	COOKING TEMPERATURE	COOKING TIME	ACCESSORY	RACK POSITION AND NOTES
Asparagus	Air Fry	400°F/205°C	4 minutes	Cooking pan	Middle position; turn partway
Beef jerky	Dehydrate	135°F/57°C	4 to 5 hours	Air frying basket on rack	Middle or highest position; set it and forget it
Beef steak	Air Fry	400°F/205°C	13 to 15 minutes	Cooking pan	Middle position; turn partway
Cake	Bake	355°F/179°C	30 minutes	Cake pan or baking dish on cooking pan	Lowest position; set it and forget it
Cauliflower florets	Air Fry	350°F/177°C	10 to 15 minutes	Cooking pan	Middle position; turn partway
Chicken, quartered	Roast	400°F/205°C	18 minutes	Cooking pan	Middle position; turn partway
Chicken, rotisserie style	Roast	380°F/193°C	45 minutes	Rotisserie spit	Set it and forget it
Chicken nuggets, frozen	Broil	400°F/205°C	10 minutes	Cooking pan	Middle position; turn partway
Chicken wings, fresh	Air Fry	400°F/205°C	10 to 12 minutes	Air frying basket on oven rack	Middle position; turn partway
Chicken wings, frozen	Air Fry	400°F/205°C	12 minutes	Air frying baskey on oven rack	Middle position; turn partway

FOOD	SMART PROGRAM	COOKING TEMPERATURE	COOKING TIME	ACCESSORY	RACK POSITION AND NOTES
Corn, on the cob	Roast	450°F/232°C	7 minutes	Cooking pan or air frying basket on rack	Middle position; turn partway
Corn dogs	Air Fry	400°F/205°C	15 minutes	Air frying basket on oven rack	Middle position; turn partway
Cupcakes	Bake	365°F/187°C	13 to 14 minutes	Silicone muffin cups on cooking pan	Lowest position; set it and forget it
Eggs, large, in shell	Air Fry	250°F/121°C	15 or 20 minutes (soft- or hard-boiled)	Air frying basket on oven rack	Middle position; set it and forget it
Falafel, frozen	Air Fry	400°F/205°C	7 to 10 minutes	Cooking pan	Middle position; turn partway
Fish sticks, frozen	Broil	400°F/205°C	10 to 12 minutes	Air frying basket on oven rack	Middle position; turn partway
Fries, fresh	Air Fry	400°F/205°C	22 to 25 minutes	Air frying basket on oven rack	Middle position; shake partway
Fries, frozen	Air Fry	400°F/205°C	12 to 15 minutes	Air frying basket on oven rack	Middle position; shake partway
Fruit leather	Dehydrate	135°F to 150°F/ 57°C to 66°C	6 to 8 hours	Cooking pan or air frying basket on oven rack	Middle or highest position; turn partway
Hash browns (patties), frozen	Air Fry	400°F/205°C	10 minutes	Air fryer basket on oven rack	Middle position; turn partway

FOOD	SMART PROGRAM	COOKING TEMPERATURE	COOKING TIME	ACCESSORY	RACK POSITION AND NOTES
Hash browns (shredded), frozen	Air Fry	400°F/205°C	10 minutes	Air frying basket on oven rack	Middle position; turn partway
Hot dogs	Air Fry	400°F/205°C	7 to 9 minutes	Air frying basket on oven rack	Middle position; set it and forget it
Mozzarella sticks, frozen	Air Fry	360°F/185°C	6 minutes	Air frying basket on oven rack	Middle position; turn partway
Muffins	Bake	350°F/177°C	15 minutes	Silicone muffin cups on cooking pan	Lowest position; set it and forget it
Nachos	Broil	400°F/205°C	4 minutes	Cooking pan	Middle position
Pizza (thin-crust), frozen	Bake	400°F/205°C	8 to 10 minutes	Cooking pan	Lowest position; set it and forget it
Potato or veggie tots, frozen	Air Fry	400°F/205°C	8 to 10 minutes	Air frying basket on oven rack	Middle position; shake partway
Salmon, fresh	Broil	400°F/205°C	8 to 10 minutes	Cooking pan	Middle or highest position; set it and forget it
Shrimp, fresh	Air Fry	400°F/205°C	3 to 5 minutes	Air fryer basket on oven rack	Middle position; turn partway
Shrimp, frozen	Air Fry	380°F/193°C	4 to 6 minutes	Cooking pan or air fryer basket on oven rack	Middle position; turn partway
Spanakopita, frozen	Bake	320°F/160°C	10 minutes	Cooking pan	Middle position; turn partway

FOOD	SMART PROGRAM	COOKING TEMPERATURE	COOKING TIME	ACCESSORY	RACK POSITION AND NOTES
Taquitos	Air Fry	400°F/205°C	10 minutes	Air fryer basket on oven rack	Middle position; turn partway
Veggie burgers, frozen	Air Fry	400°F/205°C	12 to 15 minutes	Air fryer basket on oven rack	Middle position; turn partway
Waffles, frozen	Toast	Select # of waffles	Toast Level 2	Oven rack	Middle position
White fish fillets, fresh	Broil	400°F/205°C	3 to 4 minutes	Cooking pan	Middle or top position; set it and forget it

Cooking times are a recommendation only. Always use a meat thermometer to ensure the internal temperature reaches a safe minimum temperature. Refer to the USDA's Safe Minimum Internal Temperature Chart for more information, available at https://www.fsis.usda.gov.

TIME AND TEMPERATURE CHART FOR BASKET-STYLE AIR FRYERS

FOOD	SMART PROGRAM	COOKING TEMPERATURE	COOKING TIME	ACCESSORY	NOTES
Asparagus	Air Fry	400°F/205°C	4 minutes	Air frying basket	Turn partway through cooking
Beef jerky	Dehydrate	135°F/57°C	4 to 5 hours	Air frying basket	Set it and forget it
Beef steak	Air Fry	400°F/205°C	13 to 15 minutes	Air frying basket	Turn partway through cooking
Cake	Bake	355°F/179°C	30 minutes	Cake pan in air frying basket	Set it and forget it
Cauliflower florets	Air Fry	350°F/177°C	10 to 15 minutes	Air frying basket	Turn partway through cooking
Corn, on the cob	Roast	450°F/232°C	7 minutes	Air frying basket	Turn partway through cooking
Corn dogs	Air Fry	400°F/205°C	15 minutes	Air frying basket	Turn partway through cooking
Chicken, whole	Roast	380°F/193°C	45 minutes	Air frying basket	Set it and forget it
Chicken nuggets, frozen	Broil	400°F/205°C	10 minutes	Air frying basket	Turn partway through cooking
Chicken wings, fresh	Air Fry	400°F/205°C	10 to 12 minutes	Air frying basket	Turn partway through cooking

FOOD	SMART PROGRAM	COOKING TEMPERATURE	COOKING TIME	ACCESSORY	NOTES
Chicken wings, frozen	Air Fry	400°F/205°C	12 minutes	Air frying basket	Turn partway through cooking
Cupcakes	Bake	365°F/187°C	13 to 14 minutes	Silicone muffin cups in air frying basket	Set it and forget it
Eggs, large, in shell	Air Fry	250°F/121°C	15 or 20 minutes (soft- or hard-boiled)	Air frying basket	Set it and forget it
Falafel, frozen	Air Fry	400°F/205°C	7 to 10 minutes	Air frying basket	Turn partway through cooking
Fish sticks, frozen	Broil	400°F/205°C	10 to 12 minutes	Air frying basket	Turn partway through cooking
Fries, fresh	Air Fry	400°F/205°C	22 to 25 minutes	Air frying basket	Shake partway through cooking
Fries, frozen	Air Fry	400°F/205°C	12 to 15 minutes	Air frying basket	Shake partway through cooking
Fruit leather	Dehydrate	135°F to 150°F/ 57°C to 66°C	6 to 8 hours	Air frying basket	Turn partway through cooking
Hash browns (patties), frozen	Air Fry	400°F/205°C	10 minutes	Air frying basket	Turn partway through cooking
Hash browns (shredded), frozen	Air Fry	400°F/205°C	10 minutes	Air frying basket	Turn partway through cooking
Hot dogs	Air Fry	400°F/205°C	7 to 9 minutes	Air frying basket	Set it and forget it

FOOD	SMART PROGRAM	COOKING TEMPERATURE	COOKING TIME	ACCESSORY	NOTES
Mozzarella sticks, frozen	Air Fry	360°F/185°C	6 minutes	Air frying basket	Turn partway through cooking
Muffins	Bake	350°F/177°C	15 minutes	Silicone muffin cups in air frying basket	Set it and forget it
Nachos	Broil	400°F/205°C	4 minutes	Air frying basket	Set it and forget it
Pizza (personal-size, thin-crust), frozen	Bake	400°F/205°C	8 to 10 minutes	Air frying basket	Set it and forget it
Potato or veggie tots, frozen	Air Fry	400°F/205°C	8 to 10 minutes	Air frying basket	Shake partway through cooking
Salmon, fresh	Broil	400°F/205°C	8 to 10 minutes	Air frying basket	Set it and forget it
Shrimp, fresh	Air Fry	400°F/205°C	3 to 5 minutes	Air frying basket	Turn partway through cooking
Shrimp, frozen	Air Fry	380°F/193°C	4 to 6 minutes	Air frying basket	Turn partway through cooking
Spanakopita, frozen	Bake	320°F/160°C	10 minutes	Air frying basket	Turn partway through cooking
Taquitos	Air Fry	400°F/205°C	10 minutes	Air frying basket	Turn partway through cooking
Veggie burgers, frozen	Air Fry	400°F/205°C	12 to 15 minutes	Air frying basket	Turn partway through cooking

FOOD	SMART PROGRAM	COOKING TEMPERATURE	COOKING TIME	ACCESSORY	NOTES
Waffles, frozen	Air Fry	400°F/205°C	3 to 5 minutes	Air frying basket	Set it and forget it
White fish fillet, fresh	Broil	400°F/205°C	3 to 4 minutes	Air frying basket	Set it and forget it

Cooking times are a recommendation only. Always use a meat thermometer to ensure the internal temperature reaches a safe minimum temperature. Refer to the USDA's Safe Minimum Internal Temperature Chart for more information, available at https://www.fsis.usda.gov.

TIME AND TEMPERATURE CHARTS
FOR INSTANT POT

BEANS, LEGUMES, AND LENTILS

FOOD	QUANTITY	PRESSURE LEVEL	COOKING TIME DRY*	COOKING TIME SOAKED
Black beans	2 cups +	High	20 minutes	3 minutes
Black-eyed peas	2 cups +	High	16 minutes	4 minutes
Cannellini beans	2 cups +	High	25 minutes	3 minutes
Chickpeas	2 cups +	High	35 minutes	5 minutes
Kidney beans, red	2 cups +	High	20 minutes	3 minutes
Lentils, green or brown	2 cups +	High	8 minutes	NA
Lentils, yellow, split	2 cups +	High	2 minutes	NA
Lima beans	2 cups +	High	3 minutes	1 minute
Navy beans or Great Northern beans	2 cups +	High	15 minutes	3 minutes
Pigeon peas	2 cups +	High	10 minutes	2 to 3 minutes
Pinto beans	2 cups +	High	10 minutes	2 to 3 minutes
Soybeans	2 cups +	High	35 minutes	17 minutes

*When cooking from dry, add enough water to the inner pot to cover the beans completely.

FISH

FOOD (FRESH)	QUANTITY	PRESSURE LEVEL	COOKING TIME	VENTING METHOD
Fish, fillet	1 pound	Low	1 to 2 minutes	Quick Release
Fish, whole	1 to 1½ pounds	Low	4 to 5 minutes	Quick Release

FOOD (FRESH)	QUANTITY	PRESSURE LEVEL	COOKING TIME	VENTING METHOD
Lobster tails	2	Low	2 minutes	Quick Release
Mussels	1 pound	Low	1 to 2 minutes	Quick Release
Seafood soup or stock	2 pounds	Low	7 to 8 minutes	Quick Release
Shrimp/prawn	1 pound	Low	1 to 2 minutes	Quick Release

MEAT AND POULTRY

FOOD (FRESH)	QUANTITY	PRESSURE LEVEL	COOKING TIME	VENTING METHOD
Beef, large chunks	Per pound	High	25 to 30 minutes	Natural Release
Beef, stew	Any amount	High	25 minutes	Natural Release
Beef stock or bone broth	Any amount	High	4 hours	Natural Release
Chicken breast (boneless)	Per pound	High	5 to 8 minutes	Natural Release
Chicken stock or bone broth	Any amount	High	2 hours	Natural Release
Chicken, whole	Per pound	High	8 minutes	Natural Release
Eggs, large, hard-boiled	8 to 12	High	3 to 5 minutes	Natural Release
Fish stock or bone broth	Any amount	High	30 to 45 minutes	Natural Release
Lamb, leg	Per pound	High	15 minutes	Natural Release
Pork, back ribs	Per pound	High	15 to 20 minutes	Natural Release
Pork, butt roast	Per pound	High	15 minutes	Natural Release

Cooking times are a recommendation only. Always use a meat thermometer to ensure the internal temperature reaches a safe minimum temperature. Refer to the USDA's Safe Minimum Internal Temperature Chart for more information, available at https://www.fsis.usda.gov.

RICE AND GRAINS

FOOD	QUANTITY	RICE:WATER RATIO	PRESSURE LEVEL	COOKING TIME
Barley, pearl	2 cups +	1:2.5	High	10 minutes
Congee, thick	2 cups +	1.4:1.5	High	15 to 20 minutes
Millet	2 cups +	1:1.75	High	1 to 3 minutes
Oats, quick-cooking	2 cups +	1:2	High	1 to 3 minutes
Oats, steel-cut	2 cups +	2:3	High	2 to 3 minutes
Porridge	2 cups +	1.6:1.7	High	5 to 7 minutes
Quinoa	2 cups +	1:1.25	High	1 minute
Rice, basmati	2 cups +	1:1	Low	4 minutes
Rice, brown	2 cups +	1:1	Low	20 minutes
Rice, jasmine	2 cups +	1:1	Low	4 minutes
Rice, white	2 cups +	1:1	Low	4 minutes
Rice, wild	2 cups +	1:1	Low	20 minutes

VEGETABLES

FOOD (FRESH)	QUANTITY	PRESSURE LEVEL	COOKING TIME	VENTING METHOD
Asparagus, whole or cut	Any amount	High	1 minute	Quick Release
Beans, green, yellow, or wax	Any amount	High	1 minute	Quick Release
Broccoli florets	Any amount	High	1 minute	Quick Release
Brussels sprouts, whole	Any amount	High	1 minute	Quick Release

FOOD (FRESH)	QUANTITY	PRESSURE LEVEL	COOKING TIME	VENTING METHOD
Cabbage, cut into wedges	Any amount	High	1 minute	Quick Release
Cabbage, halved	Any amount	High	3 minutes	Quick Release
Cabbage, whole	Any amount	High	4 to 5 minutes	Quick Release
Carrots, chunked	Any amount	High	1 to 2 minutes	Quick Release
Carrots, whole	Any amount	High	3 minutes	Quick Release
Cauliflower florets	Any amount	High	1 minute	Quick Release
Corn, on the cob	Any amount	High	1 minute	Quick Release
Mixed vegetables	Any amount	High	1 minute	Quick Release
Potatoes, cubed	Any amount	High	1 minute	Quick Release
Potatoes, large, whole	Any amount	High	5 to 8 minutes	Quick Release
Potatoes, small, whole	Any amount	High	3 to 5 minutes	Quick Release
Squash, butternut, cubed	Any amount	High	1 to 2 minutes	Quick Release
Squash, butternut, halved	Any amount	High	4 to 6 minutes	Quick Release
Sweet potato, cubed	Any amount	High	1 minute	Quick Release
Sweet potato, large, whole	Any amount	High	5 to 8 minutes	Quick Release

WEEKDAY MEAL PLAN AND SHOPPING LIST

MEAL PLAN

	MONDAY	TUESDAY	WEDNESDAY	THURSDAY	FRIDAY
BREAKFAST	Overnight Steel-Cut Oats	Yogurt with Chia Berry Jam	Avocado Toast with Tempeh Bacon	Grits Two Ways	Nut Butter and Banana French Toast Sandwiches
LUNCH	Turkey Monte Cristo Sandwiches	Classic Tomato Soup with Grilled Cheese Dippers	Veggie and Black Bean Quesadilla	Personal Pesto Pizzas (with store bought shortcuts)	Avocado Egg Salad Sandwiches
DINNER	Coconut Butter Chicken and Cumin Rice	Black-Eyed Pea Succotash Stew with Buttermilk Drop Biscuits (use plain butter instead of honey butter)	Whole-Wheat Spaghetti in Meaty Ragù	Veggie Meatloaf Muffins with Golden Buttery Mash	Greek Herbed Chicken Meatballs with Orzo and Chickpea Pilaf

SHOPPING LIST

FRUITS & VEGETABLES	DAIRY & EGGS	BAKERY	GRAINS, CEREALS & NOODLES	CANNED GOODS
1 pint berries (any variety, fresh or frozen)	milk (2 cups, any unsweetened/unflavored variety)	sourdough sandwich loaf (12 slices)	steel-cut oats (1½ cups)	petite diced tomatoes (2 [14.5-ounce] cans)
2½ cups frozen corn kernels	heavy cream or half-and-half (¼ cup, optional)	crusty boule or bâtard (8 thick slices)	long-grain white rice (1¼ cups)	whole peeled tomatoes (28-ounce can)
1 banana + 2 more if making sweet grits	buttermilk (½ cup)	challah or Texas toast (8 slices)	brown rice (½ cup cooked)	tomato paste (2 tablespoons)
1 lemon (4½ teaspoons juice)	sour cream (½ cup or so)	whole-wheat tortillas (4)	stone-ground grits or polenta (1 cup)	coconut milk (½ cup)
1 head lettuce (iceberg, green leaf, butter, or romaine)	5 cups yogurt (plain Greek or whole-milk)		puffed rice or cornflakes cereal (3 cups)	low-sodium vegetable or chicken broth (5 cups)
3 bell peppers	cream cheese (4 ounces)		panko breadcrumbs (1¼ cups)	
2 zucchini	butter (dairy or plant-based, 19 tablespoons)		1 pound whole-wheat spaghetti	
1 Persian cucumber	6 slices cheddar (dairy or plant-based)		orzo pasta (8 ounces)	
cherry tomatoes (1 cup)	grated or shredded parmesan (14 tablespoons)			
2 large avocados	shredded Mexican cheese blend (1 cup)			
small butternut squash (1¾ to 2 pounds)	shredded Italian cheese blend (1 cup)			
3 Yukon Gold potatoes	large eggs (9, add 4 if making savory grits)			

PROTEINS (MEATS, ALTERNATIVES & BEANS)	STORE-BOUGHT SHORTCUTS	HERBS, SPICES & SEASONINGS	OILS, VINEGARS & CONDIMENTS	BAKING AISLE, SWEETENERS, SEEDS & NUTS
1 pound ground chicken or plant-based grinds	guacamole	kosher salt	olive oil (1 cup)	all-purpose flour (3 cups)
1 pound ground turkey or plant-based grinds	salsa	flaky salt	coconut oil (¼ cup)	cornstarch (1 teaspoon)
1½ pounds boneless, skinless chicken breasts (if using for butter chicken)	pesto	black pepper	toasted sesame oil (1 tablespoon) if making savory grits	baking powder (1 teaspoon)
turkey or ham deli meat, or vegetarian deli meat (8 ounces)	marinara sauce (24-ounce jar)	whole cumin seeds (½ teaspoon)	olive or avocado oil spray	baking soda (¼ teaspoon)
tempeh (8 ounces)	pizza dough (if used, no yeast needed in pantry staples)	cayenne pepper (½ teaspoon)	apple cider vinegar (1 teaspoon)	powdered sugar (optional)
1 package firm tofu (7 ounces in recipe)		ground cumin (1 teaspoon)	sriracha or sambal oelek (1½ tablespoons, if making savory grits)	agave nectar or honey (½ cup)
chickpeas (1 can, or 3 cans if doing vegetarian butter chicken variation)		smoked paprika (1 teaspoon)	soy sauce or tamari (5 tablespoons)	maple syrup (2 tablespoons)
black beans (1 can, need ½ cup)		ground turmeric (1 teaspoon)	ketchup (¼ cup)	hemp seeds (¼ cup, if making sweet grits)
dried black-eyed peas (8 ounces)		garam masala (1½ teaspoons)	mayonnaise (3 tablespoons)	chia seeds (1 tablespoon)
		Italian seasoning (3½ teaspoons)	yellow mustard (4 teaspoons)	nut butter (¼ cup, plus another ¼ cup if making sweet grits)
		dried thyme	Dijon mustard	
		chili powder (½ teaspoon)	jam (any berry or stone fruit variety)	

FRUITS & VEGETABLES	DAIRY & EGGS	BAKERY	GRAINS, CEREALS & NOODLES	CANNED GOODS
fresh flat-leaf parsley (2 tablespoons)				
fresh mint (2 tablespoons)				
fresh cilantro (10 tablespoons)				
2 green onions (if making savory grits)				
2 carrots				
2 celery stalks				
5 yellow onions				
1 red onion				
garlic (16 cloves)				
ginger (1-inch piece)				

PROTEINS (MEATS, ALTERNATIVES & BEANS)	STORE-BOUGHT SHORTCUTS	HERBS, SPICES & SEASONINGS	OILS, VINEGARS & CONDIMENTS	BAKING AISLE, SWEETENERS, SEEDS & NUTS
		red pepper flakes (½ teaspoon)		
		ground cinnamon (½ teaspoon)		
		lemon pepper (2 teaspoons)		
		garlic powder (½ teaspoon)		
		ground nutmeg (⅛ teaspoon)		
		dried oregano (1 tablespoon)		
		everything bagel seasoning, za'atar, or toasted sesame seeds		
		liquid smoke (½ teaspoon) or smoked paprika		
		vanilla (½ teaspoon)		
		nutritional yeast (1 tablespoon)		

INDEX

Whole-Wheat Spaghetti in Meaty
Ragu, 136–37, *137*
Tzatziki Dip, Greek Herbed Chicken
Meatballs with, *152,* 153–54

V

Vegetable(s). *See also specific
vegetables*
and Barley Soup, Pantry, *68,* 69
Instant Pot time and temperature
charts, 271–72
Lentil Stew, Moroccan-Spiced, 92–93
Roasted, with Olive Oil and Garlic,
218
Steamed, with Butter and
Parmesan, 217
Super Duper Greens, 219–20, *221*
Veggie and Black Bean Quesadilla,
54, *55*

Vortex Plus basket-style air fryer, xii,
xiv

W

Walnuts
Delicata Squash and Brussels
Sprouts with, *208,* 209
Rocky Road Brownies, *236,*
237–38
Wontons
Apple Pie, *242,* 243–44
Fried, and Mango "Poke," 33

Y

Yeast, xvi
Yogurt
with Chia Berry Jam, 10–12, *11*

Greek, and Mango Cheesecake,
246, 247–48
Tzatziki Dip, *152,* 154

Z

Zucchini
Black-Eyed Pea Succotash Stew,
94–95
and Cherry Tomatoes, Focaccia
with, 187–88, *189*
and Corn, Ground Turkey Chili
Verde with, 105–6, *107*
Moroccan-Spiced Vegetable Lentil
Stew, 92–93
Roasted Vegetables with Olive Oil
and Garlic, 218
and Romesco, Blistered Green
Beans with, 213–15, *214*
Super Duper Greens, 219–20, *221*

© Aaron Blumenshine

COCO MORANTE is a recipe developer and the author of the bestsellers *The Essential Instant Pot Cookbook* and *The Ultimate Air Fryer Oven Cookbook, The Ultimate Instant Pot Cookbook, The Ultimate Healthy Instant Pot Cookbook, The Essential Diabetes Instant Pot Cookbook,* and *The Essential Vegan Instant Pot Cookbook.* Her recipes are featured in outlets such as *People,* Epicurious, TASTE, Simply Recipes, and The Kitchn. She lives in Portland, Oregon, with her husband, two daughters, and beagle.